MY MARWELLOUS LIFE

MY MARWELLOUS LIFE

In Zoos and Conservation

John Knowles OBE

Book Guild Publishing

Sussex, England

First published in Great Britain in 2009 by
The Book Guild Ltd
Pavilion View
19 New Road
Brighton, BN1 1UF

Copyright © John Knowles 2009

Second printing 2010

Typeset in Times by Ellipsis Books Limited, Glasgow

Printed in Great Britain by CPI Antony Rowe

A catalogue record for this book is available from The British Library.

ISBN 978 1 84624 365 3

To Margaret who never lost faith . . .

Acknowledgements

Without the support, practical help and encouragement of two remarkable ladies this book would never have happened.

Firstly, Gaynor Worman who worked with me at Marwell for many years as a brilliant press and public relations officer, and magazine editor. She encouraged me to shape my scattered memories into a coherent story and untangled the endless knots into which my word processor and myself had wound ourselves.

Secondly, my good friend and former Marwell Trustee, Alison Chestnutt, brought her wide knowledge of literature and proofreading skills to refining my thoughts and words, suggesting balance where needed and wisely, in some cases, toning down my more intemperate opinions.

To both I offer my sincere thanks for their hours of work and endless patience.

If a man does not keep pace with his companions,
perhaps it is because he hears a different drummer.
Let him step to the music he hears,
however measured or far away

Henry David Thoreau

Prologue

Retrospection is a luxury that I have never allowed myself. Throughout my life there has always been another mountain to conquer, another goal to seek and I hope that this will always be so. Nevertheless a brief time of looking back with satisfaction occurred in the little-known African kingdom of Swaziland in January 2008. Shortly after a flight from London via Johannesburg to the tiny but sparkling Manzini airport and a bumpy, dusty car ride, I was sipping a welcome beer in the guest cottage overlooking the wooded grassland of the Mlilwane reserve with two people with whom I shared a project which, after half a lifetime, was one of my proudest. The usual sociable enquiries into the journey and our respective states of health had barely begun when the excited voice of a Swazi ranger told us of the birth of another calf in the herd of animals which was the object of this and my previous journeys to this country.

My colleagues were Ted Reilly, the iconic leader of conservation in Swaziland, and Hamish Currie, a veterinary surgeon with a small animal practice in Constantia near Cape Town, South Africa, whose passion for wildlife had led to the creation of the Back to Africa organisation and to my presence in the park known as Mlilwane. The birth was of a Roan antelope calf whose mother had been born in Marwell Zoo which I had founded in 1969 in the south of England, with the express purpose of ensuring the survival of as many species as possible in a latter-day Noah's Ark. My hope then was that, even if an animal should become extinct in its natural home, it would not join the ranks of those, like the much-cited Dodo, which would never again share Planet Earth with mankind the most destructive of all animals. That species whose dominion has been so damaging to all

1

JOHN KNOWLES

others and frequently to itself. Back to Africa, with its aim of establishing zoo-born animals in former habitats, was a natural partner for the Marwell of my vision.

The Roan is one of the largest and most beautiful of African antelopes, and the last wild one in Swaziland died in a poacher's snare in 1961. This was at a time when conservation was the concern of very few people worldwide and of only one person in that small kingdom which, until 1968, was under British control. That one person was the aforementioned Ted Reilly who began by turning his family property of Mlilwane into a nature reserve. He did this with such success that slowly and with much encouragement from early conservationists such as the late Prince Bernhard of the Netherlands, and with the support of the King of Swaziland, he was able to develop two further parks under the banner of Wildlife Parks of Swaziland.

As the country had been virtually stripped of its native wildlife, Ted was faced not only with securing the parks from the depredations of poachers, but also with acquiring animals from outside the kingdom. This had to be done by purchasing foundation breeding populations, largely from neighbouring South Africa. Then, as now, animals there are regarded as part of the economy of both national and private game parks, unlike in the present-day zoo world. One notable exception was a male Hippopotamus bred at Whipsnade Wild Animal Park in England, which was donated by the Zoological Society of London, then under the leadership of its Director of Zoos, the late Colin Rawlins. The monetary value of wild animals in South Africa reflects their numerical status both in the wild and in captivity. The Roan is one of the least abundant species and is consequently the highest priced, so although Ted's years of work had succeeded in creating safe areas for a future return of this species to the parks in his care, the goal was financially out of reach.

During his South African military service as a veterinary surgeon, Hamish had known the Reilly family through their involvement in saving the indigenous native cattle breed known as the Nguni. This animal had been cast aside in a fashion for breeds of European origin until, thanks to Ted's pioneering work, their qualities of longevity, resistance to disease and ability to thrive in adverse conditions led to their present resurgent popularity. The long-standing friendship between

2

these two men led to Hamish's perception of the need for animals to be returned to their native homes from successful zoo-bred populations and from there to his creation of Back to Africa and his entry into my life.

I had returned to the directorship of Marwell after the departure of the person who on 12 April 2000 had succeeded me on my retirement, when my busy day was interrupted by Marwell's General Curator who wished me to meet an African veterinary surgeon who shared my passion for African hoofed animals. At first I demurred as he had no appointment and I had much to do, but I gave way, and having met him soon grew to like him as a person, and his plans. A few months later, Hamish and I spent some time in Botswana and in Swaziland where I met with Ted, saw his work and agreed that Marwell-born animals going to Swaziland was in keeping with the vision that had led me to create a zoological park more than 30 years earlier. In the 6 years since that first visit, the three of us had become friends as well as colleagues.

Somehow it seemed more than a little symbolic that so shortly after my arrival, our beers should be interrupted by the news of another Roan antelope birth. We abandoned our cool drinks and eagerly set off by Land Rover to check on the welfare of the newborn calf.

Later, trying to sleep after the buzz that always overtakes me in Africa, I pondered the strange course that my life had taken.

Chapter 1

One of the many great mysteries of life is what makes us the kind of people we are. What, for instance, made an only child, of totally normal parents, brought up in a middle-class suburban home, totally obsessive about animals from the moment he reached the age of comprehension? Such a child was the writer of this history, born in Chelmsford, Essex, in 1929.

My parents, Frank and Florence, were typical of the upwardly mobile middle class of the early 20th century. Both came from a working-class background and had risen in affluence and status by hard work and a desire to improve their own lives and that of any future offspring. My father was born late in his parents' life and gained much of his early stability from the strong influences of an older brother and sister in the Kentish village of Kennington, near Ashford. Small of stature when he left school, manual employment as a carpenter's apprentice was denied him because of his size and he eventually found humble employment washing glass and other equipment in the Chemistry Department at the nearby Wye Agricultural College. There he was encouraged to learn by the man destined to become eminent as the head of the world-renowned Rothamstead Agricultural Research Station, Sir John Russell. Following this Father moved on to a working studentship at Nottingham University. He was still a student at the outbreak of World War I and immediately joined the Sherwood Foresters Rifle Regiment. He was quickly sent to Belgium and for three years fought in the battles which resulted in such devastating human carnage. His must have been a charmed life for his only two hospitalisations were both for trench foot, that notorious condition brought on by long periods spent standing in cold and filthy water. He always said that his survival through the four years of that war was due to luck, which would not have held up had he not been transferred as a chemist to Army HQ in France to conduct research on gas warfare for the final year of the war.

Back in the civilian world, he returned to Nottingham where his studies led to him obtaining the Fellowship of the Royal Institute of Chemistry, the equivalent of a degree, but earned the hard way. From Nottingham he joined the East Anglian Institute of Agriculture, which later became the Essex Agricultural College as Essex is, arguably, not part of East Anglia. There he was to remain as head of the Chemistry Department for the rest of his working life, with one interlude during World War II when he was transferred to the Ministry of Agriculture to serve as Animal Feeding Stuffs Officer for the County of Essex. He co-authored a book on organic chemistry for agriculture students in the mid-1930s which remained a standard work into the post-war period.

My mother was proud to say that she was a Cockney, having been born within the sound of London's Bow Bells to a family that had migrated to London from rural Suffolk in pursuit of greater security than that offered by the business of my great-grandfather who was a Master Blacksmith with, unfortunately, a liking for alcohol. Grandfather shod horses in London but, long before I appeared on the scene, was driven by the growing domination of the internal combustion engine to move to Chelmsford to work as an agricultural engineer, where he suffered unemployment in the farming depression of the 1930s. Respectability was very much the order of my mother's family, with a rarely used front parlour, wherein were an organ, and an aspidistra in the window. Grandmother, a staunch Methodist, firmly believed that alcohol should never pass the lips of right-thinking folk.

I was told that my father saw my mother from his office window, fell in love and pursued her until successful. Proud of his science, he was an agnostic or an atheist depending on how he was feeling. The fact that, given their background and beliefs, my parents chose to have me baptised in Chelmsford Cathedral speaks of their desire for the much-sought-after upward mobility of those times. By the time of my birth – which I was always told was extremely difficult, thus leading to the experiment never being repeated – they were affluent enough to employ a maid for a short time, and later to send me to a private kindergarten. What a glittering, ever-upward, respectable career for their only issue they must have planned and how galling to them must have been the outcome!

There must be huge chunks of my early life, carefully provided by my caring parents, that are forgotten but there are large slices which, even at this great distance of time, I can recall with startling clarity. I can still see in my mind the horses (Judy and Bob) of the milkman and the greengrocer as though it were only yesterday. I recall the thrill of being allowed to hold Judy's reins, even if the price was running up long paths holding cold milk bottles – to the consternation of my poor parents!

Other memories crowd in as I write: an ancient tin bath full of tadpoles, aquaria full of various inhabitants from local ponds and streams, small vivaria with stick insects, cardboard boxes with silk worms progressing through their various life forms and, as I grew older, domestic rabbits and Jaunty, a Scottish terrier bitch. Like any boy of that era I had toys and, indeed, in that respect I was almost certainly spoilt, being not only an only child, but also an only grandchild with, for a long time, no rival cousins. Notwithstanding superb trains and toy soldiers with all the appropriate accompanying militaria, the toys I remember most clearly are those that comprised my very first zoo and my very first farm. The inhabitants of both these institutions were superb lead figures produced by Messrs Brittains. Unfortunately these, together with other toys, were all sold for relatively small amounts of money to finance later activities.

My strongest memories of outings were to London and Whipsnade Zoos and to Bertram Mills' Circus. I believe at this time I conceived the ambition to be an elephant keeper at London Zoo, inspired no doubt by watching the riding elephants parade back and forth with their howdahs packed with visitors young and old and the keepers sitting behind the elephants' heads like real mahouts. If that wasn't enough, the keepers even received coins for their own pockets which, when placed in the animal's trunk, were dutifully passed upwards, whilst proffered buns were consumed forthwith. I remember being much impressed by one particular animal that ignored the proffered bun, but snatched the bag held by the donor which contained many more treats and swallowed it whole!

By the time I was nine years old, Britain was at war. As the years of turmoil rolled on, food rations got smaller and this provided me with a reason to go into extensive rabbit production. I would be less than truthful if I attributed this to intense patriotism. I doubt if I recognised it at the time, but the rabbits were really my first living zoo, for while I had a healthy commercial approach to my rabbit farm (in my mind destined to fund some dimly perceived future plans) I could not resist acquiring a variety of breeds, some of which, though interesting, had dubious commercial value. So far did my pursuit of the interesting but not practicable go that I once returned from my regular haunting of the local livestock market with a pair of Guinea pigs. This was the last straw as far as my long-suffering parents were concerned. They were (fairly) willing helpers in the daily struggle to find food and housing materials for my potential contributors to the national diet, but drew the line at Guinea pigs!

Books played a large part in my development. As with many of my generation I was stirred by *Black Beauty*, and soon went on to read books about the wildlife of the English countryside, the countryside itself and about the animals of other countries both in the wild and in zoos. The weekly radio broadcasts of David Seth-Smith, 'The Zoo Man', were avidly listened to on *Children's Hour*. So why did this passionately absorbed boy not go on to study zoology or some related subject and then proceed to a life of academic distinction? The very real fact of World War II is one excuse I cling to. Certainly it disrupted school studies and, perhaps more importantly, it restricted horizons. Travel was limited to the range of a bicycle. My burgeoning rabbit business was probably a greater factor, but overall, when I look back, I see a boy yearning for the open air and real life and seeing school as being of no relevance to his future. Also, if I am honest, I see a rather rebellious lad, overly sure of himself and determined to succeed, yet with no clear vision. School holiday farm work and much reading of rather romanticised farming and countryside books pointed, however, towards rural pursuits.

Greatly to the distress of my poor parents, I refused to continue with any formal studies after achieving a very modest School Certificate (then the equivalent of present-day GCSEs) before I was 16. My parents and I were faced with the awful dilemma of what to do next.

There was a brief period when a placement as a pupil with a firm of agricultural auctioneers and estate agents was considered and abandoned for no particularly good reason that I can recall. Indeed I still occasionally indulge in fantasies which have me standing on a rostrum picking bids out of the air! I have occasionally done this for charities. Fate, however, took over at this point. A conversation between my father and a local farmer of firm but far-seeing views resulted in me starting work at a farm within cycling distance of home. Filled with rather romantic concepts of farming and my likely part in it, I began in January 1946 what was to be a significant learning experience at the feet of Tom Gemmill, my new mentor and someone to whom I owe a great deal. Tom was a member of one of the large farming families which came to Essex from Scotland during the years of agricultural depression between the two world wars and acquired farms that were losing money under traditional farming methods, but became profitable when there was a willingness to work long hours, produce milk and make use of the easy rail access to the growing nearby London market.

Tom started me on what was recognised as one of the most tedious and constant jobs of those days, which was hedge and ditch trimming, armed only with a sickle, a sharpening stone and (most importantly) a hooky stick, which is used to restrain vegetation for cutting. In retrospect I can see that this was intended as a test of my staying power, as were many other jobs such as hoeing an acre of sugar beet; all were back-breaking, often heart-aching and mind-numbingly boring. This was long before today's sophisticated machinery which has eliminated most of the tedium of farm work, and with it most employment on the land. There were, however, many high spots during the long hours in all weathers, and slowly (or so it seemed) I was entrusted with more responsible tasks.

My starting wage was £2 10s (£2.50 in today's currency) less deductions for whatever then represented National Health Insurance, for a five and a half-day week. The five-day week was still far away in the future. Milking was a seven-days-a-week job. I was entitled to one week's paid holiday but received nothing for days off, whether sick or for self-indulgence. My mother received £1 a week for my keep and I usually managed to save £1 whilst still having an active social life, centred around Young Farmers and Young Conservative clubs.

To my delight, Tom bred Suffolk Punch heavy horses which were broken to farm tasks and with which I was allowed to work. Heavy horses are very quick to learn compared, in my experience, with lighter breeds of domestic horses such as those I encountered as a volunteer at riding stables. Here a passion was born for the horse family which was to manifest itself many years later with the wild cousins of the animals of my youth. Tom allowed me to graduate to tractor driving on machines that are now seen regularly at agricultural shows as vintage exhibits. Only at the end of my learning period did we have a tractor with a self-starter. Present-day toilers on the land cannot know the dubious pleasures of starting a tractor on a damp winter's morning by swinging a handle that might, if the engine chose to fire, kick strongly enough to break a wrist!

I helped milk by hand the farm's herd of Shorthorns which, because of the need to produce milk from tuberculosis-free herds, were replaced by Ayrshire cattle at the same time as milking machines replaced aching hands. This, too, taught me a lesson because the Shorthorns, including the bulls, were easy-going compared to the Ayrshires. I learnt this first when a cow, defending her newborn calf, used her horns to throw me over a five-barred gate. Some time later Tom summoned me to help him with a bull that the senior herdsman was having trouble with. It was only because we were both fleet of foot that we escaped with our lives. Bulls were soon replaced by young men carrying thin glass tubes of life-creating semen.

As I have said, I owe Tom a great deal for what he taught me of the mixed farming of that time, which stood me in good stead when I began farming on my own. I also owe him for his role in strengthening my character and ensuring that I learnt to just plain stick at a task, however unpleasant. Our relationship can best be characterised by one occasion when he criticised me for some error. I replied cheekily that he was hurting my immortal soul, to which he responded with: 'The only soul that you have got, John, is an arsehole.'

My four years of practical farm work were interrupted by a year at the Essex Agricultural College, where my father was still teaching agricultural chemistry, a subject at which I again failed to live up to his expectations. This prepared me (more or less) to be a farmer. My time as a student was both happy and academically successful. The college had four farms with special courses available for engineering, horticulture, fruit farming and poultry farming. My general agriculture course touched on all these to a small extent. Ironically, in view of how my life was to evolve, poultry was a subject none of us took very seriously, partly because we saw it as the farmer's wife's department, and very largely because the poultry lecturer had a face and facial mannerisms more than a little like those of a frenetic farmyard cock!

Before my year at college, I had already decided that farming was to be my future. To be sure, there were days of huge discomfort with tasks like loading mud-encrusted sugar beet onto a lorry in pouring rain, but there were also glorious days of achievement such as cereal harvests in the days before the universal use of combine harvesters, when after forking sheaves of wheat onto a horse-drawn wagon, I led the full wagon back to the rick yard, successfully overcoming the all-too-clever desire of a horse to end work for the day by catching a front wheel on a gatepost, or pulling close enough to a ditch to topple the whole lot off. Harvest time in those days was also a time of fellowship, as it was one of the few times when all sections of the farm staff were involved in the same tasks. It was also a time for repetition of time-worn jokes, often at the expense of the newest members. During my first harvest I was asked with all seriousness if I was ready to participate in the ritual of 'shoeing beer', at which the newcomer had a foot held up by one person whilst another drove a nail into his boot until the sufferer shouted 'Beer', which was a commitment to buy pints for all. Although threatened with this, I managed to avoid it. Nevertheless, venturing into a local hostelry favoured by my co-workers could be financially dangerous!

Then, as now, the farming ladder was hard to get a foot on, with land being expensive and rented farms seldom becoming available. Indeed, as I learnt many years later, out of my student group only one other remained in farming and his was an inherited farm. Fate then took a kindly interest in me as she was destined to do many times in the years ahead, although not without subjecting me to long periods of trial by hardship and anxiety. A near-derelict farm near

Braintree in Essex of a mere 127 acres with no human dwellings came onto the market and, because of its dilapidated state, was knocked down to my father for a price just within his means. It was agreed that this modest, but immediately much-loved, piece of England should be rented to me at a commercial rate. A bank loan guaranteed by my father, together with my life's savings of £150 (not a small sum in those days) enabled me to start in business on Michelmas Day 1950, just seven days ahead of my 21st birthday. Michelmas Day (29th September) is the traditional day for the exchange of farms by sale or tenancy, being the end of one harvest and the beginning by new cultivations and sowings of another farming year.

The farm was only one field wide at the roadside buildings, widening, after several hundred yards of a sunken lane, which was barely navigable with a tractor in wet weather, into a series of rather small fields all surrounded by overgrown hedges and in need of drainage. An adjacent further 9 acres was rented from the Admiralty who had commandeered the adjoining property during the war for use as an American military hospital. This, then, was my beginning as a farmer and businessman at the ironically named Cut Hedge Farm.

My early years on the farm were reasonably successful as fields responded to deeper ploughing and control of overgrown hedges, weeds and rabbits. Surprisingly, in view of their present-day scarcity, we also had too many hares, with the furthest 11-acre field often having more hares than acres. Three hares can eat as much corn or grass as one sheep, so I had to face the dilemma that confronts present-day conservationists, which can succinctly be phrased as 'them or us'. I was also lucky enough to harvest a very good crop of malting barley when it was in exceptionally high demand, and sold it for a then record price, thus ensuring a healthy profit for my first year as a farmer. What a clever – and, I am sure, unbearable – young man I must have been!

Anyway, it was not long before fate decided to take another substantial interest in my affairs and bring me down to size with two wet and poor harvests and a money-losing pig enterprise, by which time I was responsible for a wife and two young sons. This was the only time in my life that I told a serious lie. This was to a corn merchant to whom I owed a great deal of money, who asked if I had any similar large debts. I assured him that his was a position of unique privilege. Had he known the truth, I would probably not now be writing this story! I still, some 55 years on, feel ashamed of that lie, although happily in time all my creditors were fully repaid with interest. Things were pretty desperate when a friend suggested that I buy, for very little money, a few exhausted battery hens and go into egg production as a means of generating a little pin money. Those scruffy hens not only rewarded me with a profusion of valuable eggs, but set me on a course that was, eventually, to take me around the world and, through a series of happy chances, lead me to the fulfilment of what were then unrecognised ambitions.

A rapid series of lucky breaks then came my way, beginning with a visit from the Essex county poultry adviser who suggested that I should expand and produce fertile eggs for a hatchery well known for its day-old chicks. For a modest amount I was able to rent a whole block of huts in the neighbouring former Admiralty-owned hospital, in what had been an entire fenced unit for recovering enemy prisoners of war. I adapted the huts, acquired breeding stock and began production. After a while, a young man who was formerly an employee of the hatchery became my poultry manager and suggested that we buy a small incubator and go into the profitable business of producing day-old chicks. This was soon accomplished. However, our first advertisement in local papers produced a warning from the hatchery to which we were selling our fertile eggs that I should stop competing with them or they would cancel my contract. Still a cocky young man, I chose independence and went to the hire purchase company for another incubator.

Our day-old chicks were well received. When I perceived a market for specially bred birds for the chicken meat market, which was emerging with the end of animal food rationing and increased prosperity in the later years of the 1950s, I was able to buy some strains of birds which, by careful cross-breeding, produced chicks with good meat conformation and growth rate, and these were soon in great demand. I knew, however, that in the United States where the war had not held back poultry production, breeding strains were being developed which had economic advantages which could not be achieved in Britain. I purchased subscriptions to American poultry magazines in order to obtain the names and addresses of all the major breeders, to whom I then wrote seeking possible future co-operation. All acknowledged my letters and sent interesting literature, but rightly pointed out that neither live poultry nor fertile eggs could be legally be imported into the UK because of poultry health regulations. Some breeders had smuggled in fertile eggs, taking advantage of the fact that Customs officials could hardly be expected to tell fertile eggs from those intended for eating. However, to achieve American standards, large numbers, together with transparency of operation, were needed.

One company had invited me and other breeders to meet a representative at the US Embassy in London. Amazingly, none of the others, all of whom were bigger and stronger than me in the hatchery business, took up the invitation and I travelled back from London with the understanding that I could be the UK franchise for the Cobb Breeding Company of Massachusetts if I could find a legal way to import foundation stock. Once more Fortune smiled on me and a talk to the senior Government Veterinary Officer for Essex led to him directing my attention to a clause in the regulations that allowed fertile egg importations from Scandinavian countries, which could themselves import fertile eggs from America into facilities of a certain standard.

Together with a Norfolk poultry breeder, Peter Beck, with whom I merged my poultry interests, we negotiated the rental of a farm near Stockholm to house one generation of American birds and we launched Cobb UK after 18 months of frantic activity. My farm did not suffer because of the years of poultry activity, and in fact benefited from the improvements that I was able to make with money generated by the humble fowl. Indeed I was then able to establish a flock of pedigree Dorset Horn sheep and a beef rearing unit. Truth to tell, I obtained much more pleasure, but much less profit, from the sheep and cattle than from the chickens. I have always found it emotionally easier to relate to mammals than to birds. Amazingly, during these years I found time to chair the local branch of the National Farmers' Union for a year and to serve on various farming-related committees.

Throughout these years my interest in wild animals grew, and gradually I had slightly more time for zoo and other animal visits. My library of related books increased in parallel with an ever-growing passion. I became an associate of the Zoological Society of London

(ZSL) which entitled me to the now commercially unbelievable privilege of visiting either London (Regent's Park) or Whipsnade Zoos before noon on Sundays, at which time ordinary visitors were admitted. I joined the Fauna Preservation Society (now Fauna & Flora International) which is the oldest British conservation organisation. Little did I know that the humble chicken would eventually lead to the second half of my life being involved professionally with wildlife and conservation, and the opportunity to serve on the councils of both the ZSL and the Fauna Preservation Society.

Chapter 2

In 1961 I travelled for the first time to the United States to learn more of the Cobb chicken and the American poultry industry, and to purchase incubators and other equipment in readiness for the arrival of the eggs from Sweden and the start of our new venture. In those days a visit to America was not the commonplace event that it has now become, and I confess to experiencing frequent feelings of awe and jealousy at seeing so much that seemed far ahead of us in a Britain still recovering from World War II. Currency for foreign travel was very restricted then, and this caused a great deal of stress to business and ordinary travellers alike. Although by this time most transatlantic flights were accomplished by planes with jet engines, some Heathrow terminal buildings were still wooden huts, and New York was the only arrival point in America from London. The morning after my arrival in the Big Apple I boarded an aircraft for Saint Louis, Missouri, where I was to connect to a flight to Fayetteville in Arkansas which was the nearest airport to the Cobb hatchery in that state.

Having several hours to await my connection, I left the Saint Louis airport and took a cab to the zoo. Such an action would probably not be possible today, as security checks would be so time-consuming that such a diversion would be pointless. In those days many of the bigger American zoos offered free admission to all. Saint Louis was one of these, and is now one of the very few American zoos still with such a policy. This reflected the commendable civic pride of cities that once perceived their zoo as a necessary cultural and recreational amenity in the same way as they would a museum, concert hall or theatre.

Sadly, I have never had an opportunity to revisit the Saint Louis

Zoo, which I believe is now a fine modern zoo in every way with an excellent record of significant financial contributions to wildlife conservation *in situ*. My impression then was of a huge collection, largely housed in late-19th-century buildings, and with circus-type wild animal shows during the summer season. I had a long chat with a keeper in the lion house, a building reminiscent of the one in London Zoo which had been much copied by zoos built in the late 19th and early 20th centuries, and which, in response to 'modernity', was demolished in 1975. I returned to the airport for my onward flight greatly enlightened by him about North American 'Zoodom' and, as ever, stimulated by what I had seen and heard.

My time in Arkansas was rewarding in a business sense. I learnt of the scale and structure of integrated poultry meat businesses, much of which was later to be copied in Britain and worldwide. The sight of a processing plant for poultry meat entirely staffed by Cherokee Indians did severe damage to my romantic views of Cowboys and Indians! There were also two unexpected effects on me personally. The first was an awareness of a very simple but warm and neighbourly hillbilly lifestyle and the second was a lifelong addiction to Bourbon whisky. It had never occurred to my host (Cobb's southern manager) that anyone drank anything else and, as I had never liked Scotch whisky, I was an easy convert. Arkansas was a very isolated state, with its citizens largely, and happily, unaware of the world beyond the state boundaries. One of the reasons for the company's very successful operation there was that the manager, the late Charlie Jones, was not just a great character in himself, but was also a local hero having left the state for six seasons in his youth to play professional (American) football for the Washington Redskins.

My travels took me to Georgia, Maryland, Milwaukee and then to the Cobb headquarters in Massachusetts. Finally I returned to New York, where I made my first visit to the Bronx Zoo of the New York Zoological Society which, much later, would change its name to the World Conservation Society to reflect its role outside its perimeter fence, with staff members working on conservation projects in over 50 countries. Two things stick in my memory from that visit. The first was a clever piece of landscaping which gave visitors the impression of lions being in the same enclosure as antelope and zebras, thus creating an attractive African panorama. The second was in the house then devoted to the anthropoid (man-like) apes, where, in a circular building, the visitor viewed chimpanzees, orang-utans and gorillas before coming to a 'cage' with very thick bars, above which was a sign that read: 'The most dangerous animal the world has ever known'. When standing in front of this one saw that it was, of course, a mirror! As with my visit to the Saint Louis Zoo, the sheer size of the Bronx Zoo amazed me and I certainly did not envisage a prospect of myself ever having a role in any zoo. Becoming a major player in poultry breeding was then my only aspiration.

After my return to Britain I had much work to do, but could not fail to be aware of just how much behind America we were. The enormous American cars with shark-like fins had power steering and automatic transmission to make light of travel on the country's vast road systems. Drive-in takeaways and other fast food outlets which would soon come to Europe then seemed a wonder. Conspicuous consumption, which we now view with disapproval, seemed very attractive to a first-time visitor from impoverished Britain. Much of what I saw is now commonplace throughout the developed world and is the subject of present-day debate as to its merits or demerits. To me in 1961 the American way of life seemed very desirable. At that time I never thought that my involvement with domesticated feathered animals would enable me to see so much more of America and the wider world.

Very soon after that, with the Anglian Hatcheries Ltd and Cobb Breeding Company (UK) Ltd companies achieving great success with the Cobb chicken, I began to agitate for the American company to grant us a greater sales area. As a result of this I was asked to travel with Ted Raymond, Cobb's American vice-president for sales, to South Africa and Rhodesia. Ted had arranged for our journey to begin in Amsterdam and, to my surprise, the journey was in a propeller-driven plane. Ted explained that Africa clearly would not have runways capable of handling jet-engined planes. Our first refuelling stop was in Kano in Northern Nigeria, where our plane was surrounded by the jet-engined monsters of that time! Flying into South Africa with its policy of apartheid, we had long immigration forms to complete which included the question: 'What European languages do you speak?' My American colleague wrote: 'None'!

Protectionism by the established breeders in South Africa, who had invited us and who were extremely hospitable, ensured that we had no business success. Not for the last time was I to come across animal health regulations designed to protect established local breeders from their more efficient competitors in other countries. Exactly the same courteous and friendly approach to us was used to explain in great detail the sound reasoning behind the apartheid policy, then so dominant in all aspects of life in the Republic, and the benefits that this was bestowing on those without white faces. At almost the same time, my exposure to the United States brought me face to face, for the first time in my life, with the tensions that can exist between races. In many ways an African American was then treated in those southern states as a lower life form. By this time, we in Britain had experienced immigration of non-whites from former British territories and had heard Enoch Powell's warnings of 'Rivers of Blood', but that had not made much impact on a country boy like me.

Although the Cobb headquarters was in the liberal state of Massachusetts, over the years most of the production of poultry meat had moved away from the colder climates of the northern states. Firstly it went to the Delmarva (parts of the states of Delaware, Maryland and Virginia) Peninsula, where growers were seeking alternative sources of income due to the loss of their garden produce market in the big cities of the East Coast, as a result of airfreight bringing in more cheaply produced fresh fruit and vegetables from California and Florida. Chicken meat seemed to be one possible alternative. Initially they sought to use their glass houses, but these proved unsuitable and were replaced by purpose-built buildings. For a time this poultry industry prospered, as with horticultural produce, because of proximity to the large urban conurbations of the East Coast. However, changing times and lower costs had caused most production to move to southern states where costs were lower because of cheap freight access to the huge grain-producing areas of the American Corn Belt which provided the larger part of poultry food ingredients.

It was in those southern states that I experienced racism at its angriest. This was after the time of the desegregation struggle, begun by a brave lady determined to ride in a 'Whites Only' section of a crowded bus. It was a time of riots in big cities, passionate speeches by the soon-to-be-assassinated Martin Luther King and emergent, but struggling, legislation. The American Civil War was only a century old and was still being 'fought' by many. After a few drinks any group of 'good ol' boys' could be guaranteed to be telling anti-black jokes, whilst many of the more staid community members would fly the flag of the Old Republic at their house or on their boat.

With our US headquarters near very liberal Concord, Massachusetts, the home of the poet-philosophers Ralph Waldo Emerson and Henry David Thoreau, and of the author of *Little Women*, Louisa May Alcott, it is hardly surprising that there then was a distinct philosophical divide amongst North and South staff, into which I fitted neatly as a 'non-combatant'. I soon learnt that the phrase 'Gone with the Wind', which referred to all that had preceded America's civil war, was only partially true and that the spiritual divisions remained.

From South Africa I flew to the Rhodesian capital of Salisbury, now Harare, where I made a franchise agreement with an established poultry business, the owner of which was later to become a minister in Ian Smith's government, after it had declared UDI (unilateral independence). This denied us our royalties because of sanctions. In an effort to recoup some of this money, with the help of our finance director, I set up a Rhodesian company with the intention of using our locked-in funds to invest in land. On returning to Britain we were told that our actions were illegal and that we could be liable to imprisonment. Being far too busy to have time to rest at Her Majesty's expense, we quickly unscrambled the new company, and no benefit ever came from that particular African business.

That brief time in Rhodesia turned me into an Afrophile. I had but one short visit to a wildlife park and one Sunday on a friend's farm, but this was enough for me to develop a true feeling of belonging. Happily the future was to bring me many times to the African continent, though not, eventually, as a poultry man. In Rhodesia there was nothing like the oppressive philosophy and reality of apartheid that existed in its southern neighbour, South Africa. The only barrier that stopped a non-white going anywhere was an economic one. With the country then so rich in good farming land, minerals and wildlife, and with more water than much of Southern Africa, it had enormous appeal to me. To this day I am not sure why I did not abandon my plans and emigrate to this wonderful place. However, I chose to pursue my ever-more ambitious desires to populate the world with our fast-growing chickens.

My next expansion opportunity arose when Cobb America, who held the master franchise, rather grudgingly allowed the English company to try to sell to the USSR where we went to a government-sponsored British Agricultural Exhibition, staged in the grounds of the Park of Soviet Economic Achievements. The venue was as depressing as its name suggests. Still more depressing was the Hotel Ukraine in which we were billeted. This was one of the four so-called wedding cake buildings which Stalin had built dotted in a square formation around central Moscow. The rooms were dreary to say the least with, as was always the case in the Communist world, no plugs for either the bath or the hand wash basin. Each of the 20-plus floors was watched over by a grim-faced harridan who grudgingly handed our keys back and forth as we came and went. The vast building had been built without adequate lifts so that it was necessary to leave your room at least half an hour before any appointments in the lobby. The alternative of walking down was not an option as there was at least one 'non-floor' – which we were all convinced were listening areas, linked, we were sure, to our rooms. It would be fair to say that we were all slightly paranoid, and I had hardly helped myself by reading John le Carre's *The Spy Who Came in From the Cold* during my flight from London.

Nevertheless, we were constantly buoyed up by the hope of huge contracts, guaranteed by the British government, to feed the Soviet people with chicken. This would be triggered by the eagerly awaited, but tantalisingly unscheduled, day when President Nikita Khrushchev would visit and be dazzled by British agricultural technology. There were endless rumours and much speculation as to which would be the day when the great man would come, and more than a little planning to upstage whatever competition there might be from companies with similar offerings. As we anticipated how the great man would behave towards us we remembered the televised and much publicised fierce debate that Nikita had with the American Vice-President Richard Nixon at an exhibition in Moscow of American domestic appliances. They had come as close as diplomacy allowed to fisticuffs over the merit or otherwise of the lifestyles of their respective peoples.

On the day before the end of the show the President came with his retinue, and we were the second stand on his tour. The first, which was selling incubators and processing equipment, clearly bored the great man who, for all his present eminence, was as we were to learn a peasant at heart. He crossed the passage to us with a fierce look on his face that immediately set me contemplating the wastes of Siberia. This fear was heightened when, as my team and I sprang into our rehearsed programme, I handed him a cock bird, whilst explaining that this was a male of our male line. Before I could move on to talk about the female line, he snatched the bird from me and through his interpreter told me that I was a liar, as this was a female because it had no floppy comb. Heart in mouth I explained that as our birds were initially from the cold winter climate of New England they had been bred not to have the traditional combs because these were susceptible to frostbite. He then turned the bird over, pretended to examine its sexual equipment and returned the bird to me and with great smiles said I was right. Thankfully I resumed my spiel, concluding by asking if the President would accept a trio of our birds as a gift. The answer was a gracious and predictable acceptance which, in the tradition of such things, I did not expect to be followed up. However, to our surprise some half an hour later a rather scruffy individual came round with a cardboard box for Mr Khrushchev's chickens. The next day, the last of the show, I received a visit from a well-dressed Russian who spoke fluent English and introduced himself as the President's agricultural adviser. He asked for a diet sheet for the trio of birds, which we happily supplied, and asked if I would like a photograph of the little event of the previous day, bearing Mr Khrushchev's signature. I accepted with thanks.

Since then that picture has hung in the downstairs cloakroom of wherever I have lived. Copies were made for other parts of the Cobb empire, but inevitably the whole thing had slipped my mind when, some 44 years on, I received a phone call from a man who I had taken onto the company's payroll just before the Moscow event. He asked for details of my Khrushchev experience and whether the signature on the photo really was Nikita's. He then told me of an awakening interest in all things related to the Cold War and of a museum in Fairfax, Virginia dedicated to that era, on the board of which is a son of Nikita Khrushchev, now an American citizen. At the museum there is a copy of the picture and with it is biographical information about myself, which, he added, is also in many archives about the same period. The curator of that museum, he told me, is a son of Gary Powers, the pilot of the U2 spy plane which was shot down over Russia and caused yet another diplomatic upset during that era of strained East–West relations. It is an irony that the sons of those two men should now be collaborating.

Some four months after our meeting, Khrushchev was deposed. I doubt if this was the cause, but in spite of a number of meetings with British suppliers of specialist poultry feeds and equipment and large building contractors with a view to building a massive meat production complex in Russia, and visits by myself and others to the Soviet Embassy in London, no business arose from our endeavours. I have always hoped, however, that our three chickens may have afforded the former leader of the non-free world some interest as he wandered, lonely and forgotten, around his retirement dacha.

Our meeting was for me personally and for the British company, of which I was a 50 per cent owner, a major PR success. It led to the American company forming a very positive view of its British associates and on my second visit to the United States I was treated as something of a hero. Significantly, this was a time when our once little company was thriving, and the American originators of the bird were not doing well in any markets under their control. Furthermore, as a family business they were confronted with a number of personality and policy conflicts. From casual conversations in the autumn of 1964 merger talks began, and with them a series of fortuitous and unpredictable events which were to lead me to where my passions truly lay.

In 1966 the British and American companies merged into a company that, for tax purposes, was based in Delaware. The fact that the merger eventually proved unsuccessful is not really relevant to the story of my eventual career change. However, there is a salutary lesson to be learned from this. Because the merger negotiations were prolonged with a great deal of time taken up with writing a 'divorce' provision which could be activated by either national constituent of the new entity after two years, we had built in a self-fulfilling prophesy. This made the eventual demerger inevitable, as both parties had spent too much time ensuring their position if the divorce option was activated, rather than wholeheartedly building the merged business. For me, although I did not know it at the time, the new responsibilities taken on as a result of the merger set me onto a path of travel and experience without which my life would not have taken the course it did.

Although there had never before been a formal division of duties between Peter Beck and myself, in practice sales, marketing and strategy had been my sphere whilst the very practical Peter took care of buildings, equipment and transport. This, as far as Britain and Ireland were concerned, remained in place, but I assumed a strategic role for North America, and an overall role for Europe, Africa, the Middle East and the Indian subcontinent. The possibilities for zoo visits and wildlife experiences were not a consideration of mine when taking on these duties – but were not unnoticed either!

It so happened that the first major tour which my new role called for ended in Sri Lanka (then still Ceylon) where we already had a small distributor of our chicks, and it was here that I had an experience that shaped my future thoughts and which I liken to Paul's experience on the road to Damascus. Arriving in Colombo with no commitments for an afternoon, I decided to visit the zoo, which appealed not only because of my ever-present interest in animals but also because of its historic interest. Originally it had been designed and managed by a member of the famous German family of Hagenbeck, who in 19th-century Hamburg had pioneered open-air enclosures for wild animals with the use of moats and artificial rock work. Here I was shown a baby elephant with gunshot wounds and was told that its mother had been killed by a planter who lived about 100 miles away. The next morning our associate took me to meet his largest outlet (customer size was very small compared to Europe), and somehow that man mentioned during the usual long-drawn-out preliminaries to business discussions that he was the elephant slayer. Notwithstanding rules about getting along with customers, I must have shown my revulsion for he immediately beckoned me to follow him outside to view what had once been a 25-acre field of sugar cane which had virtually been destroyed by wild elephants, with only a few portions (those which would have been viewed daily) left untouched. The elephants had learnt to hide their depredations from humans. As my host was quick to point out, this had implications for his family which he could not overlook. The sugar cane crop was expected to provide 75 per cent of his family's income for a year.

This forced me to face the reality of wildlife versus human conflict that was just beginning to gain the recognition that it would receive in future decades. Destruction of species was not just the action of greedy men. Conservation could not be achieved by simply taking away the guns and traps of poachers and persuading fashion-conscious ladies not to wear fur coats. Whilst my sympathies might lie then, as now, with the animals, the reality is and was that the dominant species on Planet Earth was expanding both numerically and in its per capita demand for resources. The most that could be hoped for was a form of compromise, and I did not need a crystal ball to see where the bargaining advantage lay. For some life forms latter-day Arks would be needed. For the most part, however, the many people I met in my travels were either not interested in the problem or felt it was too complex for them to comprehend.

My zoo visits were made opportunistically. At a World Poultry Science Association meeting held during three very hot weeks in Kiev in the Ukraine, I suffered all manner of discomforts, including personal luggage lost in Moscow airport for ten days. Each member of our delegation had one day off during this gruelling exercise and was free to choose how they spent that day, providing it was organised by the ever-watchful staff of the state tourist organisation, Intourist. In our case the Intourist staff members were all female and, one could be forgiven for imagining, chosen for having charms that might tempt a lonely foreigner. My group was so paranoid at being in a police state where these charmers held our return tickets and passports that our only thoughts were to pester them about our documents and about when we might escape. Notwithstanding our concern (which they had no doubt noted), when our departure days arrived we each received an envelope containing passports and tickets and a sad little verse that read: 'We are not loved, we are not kissed, we are the girls of Intourist'.

However, the Intourist staff were always cheerful and as helpful as the system would allow. When my turn for a day's outing arrived and I asked to go to the zoo, my request was met with gales of laughter and remarks about zoos being for children (unwelcome words that have dogged me for most of my life). Anyway, after a few explanatory words from me I was taken seriously. Rather too seriously as it turned out, for I was met by the Director and most of his staff and they asked my opinions on all manner of points including how to manage trimming the toenails of their one female Asian elephant. This animal, in the bad tradition of wild animals as gifts by heads of states, had been a gift from Indian Prime Minister Pandit Nehru. Mostly, these were questions that I was either unable to answer or where I felt that the truth would be insulting to my hosts. An inspection of the zoo hospital with its much-holed concrete floor and flaking ceiling left me feeling that it would be unwise to cut my own toenails there! My overwhelming memory from that zoo visit was of a large number of European brown bears living in very small octagonal cages, wherein were to be seen elderly Ukrainian ladies sweeping the floors around the somnolent animals. Babushkas, it seemed, were expendable! Clearly not all zoos were suitable for the role of a modern Ark!

The 1960s and early 1970s saw a slow increase in prosperity, both in Britain and throughout the non-Communist world. With greater prosperity came more leisure time and more demand for entertainment. In Britain, theme parks began to appear and animal attractions of various types emerged. Mostly these were driven solely by the desire to make a quick buck. An enterprising man started a number of zoos under a kind of franchise system, of which all but two failed to survive; these two owed their success to the fact that the owners of the land were strong enough financially to absorb the whole enterprise and operate it themselves. One that was born in this way and has survived to become a highly creditable animal collection is the Cotswold Wildlife Park.

Dolphin and killer whale shows proliferated, including one in London's Piccadilly where dancers could gyrate on glass above the animals. Such was the craze for marine attractions that, in an effort to boost visitor numbers, the Zoological Society of London unwisely committed money which was much needed elsewhere to the establishment of a dolphin show at Whipsnade. In 1966 came the opening of Longleat Safari Park, billed as the world's first 'drive-through lion park', although it had in fact been preceded by one in Pietermaritzburg in South Africa. Safari parks soon spread around the world and Jimmy Chipperfield, of the famous circus family, whose brainwave Longleat was, soon found himself entering into many deals which used his expertise and animals. It had quickly became obvious that there was sufficient interest in these parks to warrant adding other species, so gradually giraffe, zebras and antelope species were added in additional enclosures. To fill these areas, catching operations were carried out in East Africa on a scale not seen since the great collecting expeditions of the late 19th century. Much of this was managed by the Chipperfield organisation in various associations with the established animal dealers of Europe and North America and, surprisingly, considering the politics of the time, with a Communist-funded zoo in what was then Czechoslovakia. Although not motivated by any considerations of conservation, some benefits to species conservation were to emerge from this activity.

I watched all of this happening from a (sometimes jealous) distance. My time was more than taken up with affairs of business and I could only read, listen and occasionally take my long-suffering family to Sunday lunch at London Zoo. Near to my English base, in Braintree, near Colchester, Essex, a lone entrepreneur named Frank Farrar bought a 36-acre semi-derelict property with a large ugly Victorian house and outbuildings in the centre, and without the tedium of seeking planning consents that were to so afflict me a few years later, proceeded to build a zoo. With very great interest I watched from close by, although still with no view to doing something like this myself. I became something of a confidant of Frank's over the years and found to my surprise that when it came to knowledge of wildlife I often knew more than he did. Observing how the zoo developed was to be valuable to me in later years, especially when Marwell was about to become a reality. There I learnt something of the management of crowds at bank holidays and the all-important management of cars and coaches. There are tedious but vital tasks which zoo management calls for, and one of these is ensuring that cars are parked speedily so that no potential visitors and their much-needed cash are lost. Slow-moving queues are likely sources of such loss, and cars parked so that the departing visitor is trapped in are very bad for the long-term good relations on which a zoo depends. An unpaid internship in car parking was thus a valuable experience. Truth to tell, the Colchester Zoo of that time was a far from estimable institution, with its owners limited in vision but overly financially aware. When the Farrars retired, the zoo was sold to a niece of Frank's and her husband, who have since transformed it into one of Britain's finest, with some of the money generated there being invested in Africa.

My first opportunity to get really close to the world of zoos happened, as did so much of my life before and after, with what I choose to call serendipity. Together with Bobby Cobb, the son of the founder of the Cobb Breeding Company, I had been visiting our operations in Arkansas and Georgia and participating in a series of meetings in Washington, from where we travelled back to Boston which was close to our American headquarters in Concord, Massachusetts. Changing planes in New York, we delayed whilst Bobby tried without success to phone his sister, then a 'resting' Broadway actress, with a view to getting free tickets for a show. Bobby, although from a wealthy aristocratic Boston family, was always (to put it mildly) given to 'squeezing a dollar until it screamed'. As this diversion failed, we took a flight to Boston which was delayed after we left the terminal in a way that I have never experienced before or since. I could see from where I was sitting that we were spending a great deal of time moving around the taxi-ways of JFK airport, and this went on until finally a van showed up with a large 'FOLLOW ME' sign on its rear, which led the disoriented pilot to the take-off runway!

This incident resulted in our arrival in Boston being too late for a return to Concord, so a meal in a seafood restaurant near the harbour was decided upon. Entering the restaurant's bar for a preprandial drink or two, we found just one customer, discussing politics with the barman. Ever a political animal, Bobby joined in this and after a short time whispered to me that he thought this guy was an economist, probably from Harvard University, and suggested that we invite him to join us for dinner. As we had been travelling together for some five days, something which will test any relationship, I readily agreed. Upstairs at a table we introduced ourselves formally and to my amazement it emerged that the 'economist' was Walter Stone, the director of the two Boston zoos. The way Bobby tells it – and happily we are still good friends – no one spoke to *him* for some hours!

I was leaving for London the next day, but as we parted it was arranged that I would get together with Walter on my next trip to the Boston area, which was some three months later in 1966. So began a very significant friendship which opened doors and realised visions without which I might well have been a chicken man for the rest of my working life. Sadly the friendship was destined to be short-lived as Walter was killed in a car accident before I embarked on a totally new way of life. Ours was a truly life-changing friendship for me, and I hope a happy one for him.

Chapter 3

The first day Walter and I spent together was, despite a New England snowfall so huge that I had to dig my car out of the car park of the Howard Johnson Motel in Concord in order to make the dangerous journey, to the smaller of the two Boston zoos at Stoneham where Walter and his family lived in a 'zoo house'. The snowfall had been so heavy that I was halfway through my initial digging before I realised that I was working on the wrong car! This taught me always to remember exactly where I left a car during snowy weather!

Older than I by some four years, Walter had served in the American forces in Europe during World War II and, after honourable discharge, took advantage of the educational opportunities being offered to veterans and earned a degree in zoology. This led to a student curator's post at the Audubon Park Zoo, followed by the post of Curator of Mammals at the Detroit Zoo before being appointed to the Boston directorships. He must have taken this post with huge optimism because the Stoneham Zoo was to be almost completely rebuilt. Money was also promised for the larger main zoo at Franklin Park, situated in what was then one of the less salubrious parts of Boston. Both zoos at that time offered free admission to visitors. Sadly, much that was hoped for did not materialise. Both zoos were owned and operated by the Metropolitan District Commission (MDC) of Boston, with support given by a zoological society. I never got to the bottom of the difficulties between these two organisations, but Walter was caught in the middle. Furthermore, he did not enjoy a good relationship with the Commissioner for many reasons, one of which was Walter's forthright criticism of the work of the architect who had designed the Stoneham Zoo. Some of these deficiencies were pointed out to me on that very first visit as we began a friendship which would also be – although neither of us knew it at the time – partly one of teacher–pupil. I was, for example, shown the brand new giraffe house which was built in such a way that an adult visitor's eyes were level with the giraffes' knees. Now a giraffe is an impressive animal if looked up to from the ground, and also when looked at either from above or at head level, but its knees are not very impressive. Cages for many other animals were designed with equally little concern for either the inhabitant or the would-be viewer.

Another reason that we connected so well was that, just as Walter was becoming disenchanted with the way his professional life was going, I too was becoming frustrated by the Cobb businesses on both sides of the Atlantic. Truth to tell, we were also both taking too much alcohol on board and this fired our passionate denunciations of the wrongs that we were suffering and the mess that was the world in general. As I was at that time very regularly in Massachusetts, and as I almost always had free weekends, we saw a great deal of each other and we began going on trips intended for our joint pleasure and for my edification. The fact that I had access to a company car and that Walter was not the most proficient of motorists (he wrote off at least two MDC cars in the time that I knew him) was another factor in our times together.

One day at the Franklin Park Zoo Walter and I were in a stall with an Asian cow elephant while Walter discussed some problem with her keeper. As they talked, I became aware that the animal was shifting her weight almost imperceptibly so that with one quick move she could crush me against a concrete wall. A quiet move on my part ensured my survival, but it was very obvious from the look she gave me that for some reason I was *persona non grata* with that grey lady! I have never been directly concerned with elephant management but, like most animal people, find them vastly intriguing both as individuals and as species (African and Asian). African elephants are the only ones that I have observed in the wild. That little incident placed a marker in my mind which said that these are not just big, grey, loveable beasts, but they have strong individual characters with distinct likes and dislikes. On that day I obviously came into the latter category!

One of our expeditions took us north to New Hampshire, to visit a now defunct leisure attraction known as Benson's Wild Animal Farm, which was a combination of zoo and carnival (American for fairground) with thrill rides and also circus-type wild animal shows as added attractions. My interest in animals over many years had led to many visits to circuses, as well as to zoos. Properly presented, a circus show, filled with colour and music designed to excite the senses, can be a stirring experience. The sight of a large number of brightly harnessed and plumed liberty horses performing directional changes to the sound of a band playing a Sousa march has always quickened my senses. The question of performing wild animals is a different and far more complex one. I have long sought to make up my own mind on this very controversial topic, with copious reading and discussion with people who have had direct experience. However, my less than conclusive opinion is that, as in all walks of life, there are compassionate and caring animal trainers, and there are others who see it just as a job to be carried out with as little stress to human and animal alike as possible. Sadly, there are also a few sadists. With lions, tigers and leopards, training methods have varied greatly. European methods have traditionally been the more acceptable with an emphasis on good relationships between trainer and trainee and not on animal savagery with a pistol-firing 'hero' demonstrating his courage in the face of well-rehearsed danger. I do not believe that anyone is going to beat a lion or a tiger and survive into the old age that most wild animal trainers achieve, so the training of big cats is necessarily somewhat subtler than that of primates and elephants. With chimpanzees, training always begins with young animals; they are more mischievous than small children but physically stronger. To make these animals perform at set times and for a set time slot within a programme demands a level of discipline which I believe to be quite unacceptable. In America I have heard of broken limbs inflicted by a trainer whose frustration led to temper and complete loss of self-control.

These reflections are stimulated by the memory of that New Hampshire visit, when we watched an amazingly slick elephant act in which six juvenile Asian elephants performed a series of manoeuvres at speed, with the trainer standing, apparently uninvolved, by the ringside. As the elephants left the arena, Walter, who always seemed

33

to be on jovial good terms with everyone we met, went over to speak to the trainer and to introduce me. After the usual pleasantries I congratulated the elephant master and asked him how he had been able to train his animals to perform so adroitly without him being near them. With a slight smile he produced an electric prod from his pocket and said: 'They know I have this with me. Without it they would not do a thing.' This gave me much food for thought about elephants, whether in zoos, circuses or, as I had once seen in Sri Lanka, carrying out the centuries-old tasks of timber movers.

On another Saturday we took the wonderfully convenient Eastern Airways shuttle (now long since defunct) from Boston's Logan Airport to New York's La Guardia, from where we embarked on a marathon of zoo experiences. Our first (my second) visit was to the Bronx Zoo where, in his historic office, we met a man who by his personal kindnesses to me and through his writings and lectures was destined to be one of the major professional influences on my later life. This was Bill Conway, the Director of the New York Zoological Society. Under his guidance the Society not only owned one of the great zoos of the world, but also became one of the largest and most effective of global conservation bodies. Its workers research problems and provide solutions on the ground on every continent, and publish influential both popular and scientific books.

Bill had a meteoric rise in the zoo world, earned by a prodigious amount of work and by knowledge gained and, most importantly, retained. Over the years that I have known him he has never failed to amaze me with the breadth and detail of this knowledge. One moment he can be discussing some complex problem with the Chinese Giant panda management, and the next pointing out a female bird that had failed to breed for two seasons. At this first meeting, mustachioed and as usual smartly dressed in a manner slightly reminiscent of the former British Foreign Secretary and Prime Minister, Anthony Eden, he took us firstly to the basement of the administration building where he had in quarantine a group of the diminutive mouse deer of Asia. He was delighted to tell us that the group had evaded the normal quarantine for ruminants in the US government facility at Clifton (which, lacking in the caring skills needed for small animals, would almost certainly have killed them). Their import papers had named them, quite believably to a layman (because of their small size), as rodents. We moved on together to visit just a few parts of the zoo, as our schedule, set by Walter, was a fierce one. I clearly remember that in the lion house Bill remarked on an enormous tiger that he had seen somewhere belonging to an animal dealer and circus trainer from Florida. It was the first that I had heard of Siberian tigers in captivity, but it planted a seed that would later lead to another journey and a momentous decision.

All too soon we had to leave Bill and the Bronx and take a cab to downtown New York and the Central Park Zoo. This visit did not take long as it was merely an object lesson in what a zoo should not be. Built during President Franklin D. Roosevelt's schemes to lift America out of the Depression of the 1930s, and operated as a free attraction by the city of New York, it was awful. In fact, as I left it I commented that it must have been designed by a prison architect on his weekend off! Happily, a few years ago the city asked the New York Zoological Society to take over this and its other small zoos, with a substantial grant for refurbishment, and it is now a model of what a small urban zoo should be.

At the Central Park Zoo we were met by another of Walter's friends, Claude Coates, the Director Emeritus of the Aquarium on Coney Island which, despite the connotations of its location on a famous Big Apple playground, is a serious research-based public facility also owned by the New York Zoological Society. Here I was particularly impressed by my first ever viewing of a group of Beluga whales with their very blatant sexuality and 'Persil whiteness'.

Thereafter the day slipped into something of a blur, which I would like to attribute to tiredness and the absorption of so much new knowledge, rather than to the hospitality Claude gave us at an Italian restaurant where he was clearly a much-favoured customer because, although it was closed for a wedding reception, we were admitted as honoured guests. I do remember a wedding scene much like that in *The Godfather* film, and I can just about remember dancing with and kissing the bride, but of our return cab ride to La Guardia and flight back to Boston, I can only think that some kindly spirit took care of us!

In his enthusiasm to induct me into the American zoo world, Walter

used his position as a former president of the American Association of Zoos & Aquariums to insert me into the programme of that body's annual meeting held that year in Pittsburgh. I was offered a slot in which to give a paper, and rather foolishly accepted. I gave a poorly reasoned and poorly delivered contribution on how the intensive growing of chickens could reduce the demand for meat from wild animals, and thus assist in their survival. This was received in a silence more polite than it deserved. The underlying philosophy was not as crazy as it may now seem. All of us working in the Cobb family of companies hoped that the results of our researches might help meet a need for protein in the many parts of the world where human beings were suffering varying degrees of malnutrition, the very countries where wildlife was most at threat. That those poor countries still today remain malnourished is a tragic fact born of issues so complex that a discussion of them has no place here. Suffice it to say that poverty and conservation problems were then and always will be inextricably linked.

I am now often asked how I feel about the present-day much-criticised welfare aspects of modern poultry meat production. There is no doubt in my mind that its very cheapness and abundance has had a significant role in improving human diets worldwide, and the question must also be asked as to where the meat would have come from without chickens and turkeys. Certainly some would be from wild animals, as we are seeing with the current 'bush meat' crisis in West African countries where wild animals are hunted and transported to populated areas, as relatively fresh meat, by lorries travelling over roads cleared for them to carry the products of both legal and illegal logging. The counter-argument to this is that poultry are fed on largely cereal-based diets that could have been eaten directly by impoverished humans. As to the welfare aspects of modern broiler production (with which I have had no connection for over 35 years), I am amazed at the rate of weight gain that now results from the work of breeders and diet formulators since my years of involvement in the industry. That these now result in reduced animal welfare is a sad reflection on the pressures for profit to which all links in the supply chain are subject.

Although I did not cover myself with any kind of glory in Pittsburgh,

I made professional colleague acquaintanceships that were to be long-lasting and valuable as well as pleasurable. One of them, the animal dealer Fred Zeehandelaar, was soon destined to render me a great kindness. The President of the American Association of Zoological Parks & Aquariums (AAZPA) for that year was a young man who had yet to achieve the status of Director, being then the curator of a modest-sized zoo in upstate New York but soon to be appointed to lead the Denver Zoo into the modern zoo era. This was Clayton Freiheit, whom I was destined to meet many times over the coming years. Clayton was the most complete zoo manager I have ever known. He knew, and was on top of, every aspect of his zoo and was also well versed in what was happening in the wider zoo and conservation world. Like me he was passionate about Africa and its animals. Sadly he was to die in 2007, whilst still in harness at the age of 69.

Our next outing – also a very long day – was one of the most important of my life. Again it was an early morning departure from Boston, for a car ride of some five hours to the Catskill Mountains in upstate New York and the Catskill Game Farm, where we were received with great warmth by the owner, the late Roland Lindemann, and his family. Subsequent to this first visit I received much hospitality and friendship at Catskill, where I embarked on a steep learning curve. Roland and I could hardly have been more different in our backgrounds and life experiences, yet we clicked from that first meeting, to my great long-term advantage. Roland was born in Munich between the two World Wars where his father was a keen student of nature and a friend of the famous German zoo family of Heck, two brothers of which were then in charge of the Munich and Berlin zoos respectively. Among their many claims to fame, they initiated attempts at those zoos to recreate the extinct wild horses and cattle of Europe, the Tarpan and the Auroch, using existing wild and domestic species and breeds to produce reasonable likenesses of the lost animals, although to my mind they only succeeded in demonstrating the sad truth that extinction is for ever.

Early in his life, like so many Europeans, Roland came to New York to seek his fortune, a quest in which he succeeded so well that, like many affluent dwellers in the Big Apple, he was able to purchase a large property in the Catskill Mountains to which his family could retreat to escape the oppressive heat of the city during the summer months. Here, following his father's interests, Roland established some herds of semi-tame deer for the private delight of the family. These became an unexpected attraction to mountain residents and visitors, who became so numerous that their cars sometimes blocked Roland's access to his own property. Ever awake to business opportunities he decided to charge an admission fee and develop a small tourist attraction.

This was an acorn from which a great oak grew. By the time of my first visit, the Catskill Game Farm was home to the largest collection of ungulates (hoofed animals) in America and almost certainly in the world. Here I saw for the first time many different species of antelope and deer, wild species of sheep and goats, and also wild members of the horse family, most notably amongst the latter the Przewalski's wild horse, then only just declared extinct in the wild. Unlike many of the larger traditional zoos, this was no 'postage stamp collection' of as many species as possible, but maintained animals in large groups which were breeding with such success that they had not merely become self-sustaining, but had increased so as to be able to supply other zoological collections and could, if needs be, ensure the survival of a species.

It took much more than this first visit for me to take in all that was being accomplished here and how it was being achieved. From early on the park had generated an income stream and, helped by Roland's other business incomes, these monies had been invested in purchases from those engaged in the live catching of animals at a time when this was still acceptable, and from zoos, many in a Europe recovering from World War II and in need of finance. Most zoos then were yet to share the vision of species custodianship already embraced by Catskill. The important Przewalski's herd had come, as had other animals, from Munich, probably through that old family connection. It was no coincidence that a Heinz Heck became Roland's curator.

I recognised from my first visit that another aspect of Roland's creation was a very keen appreciation of visitor needs. Children were catered for with not just the tame animal petting corner then so common in zoos, but in a huge area filled with young sheep, goats and deer which could be bottle-fed for a price. There were in fact three relays of these young animals at any one time, with staff trained to see that

38

no youngster was overfed and that a member of the next relay was ready for a bottle from the clamouring children. This area was at the far end of the park, up a slight rise, which the kindly Mr Lindemann had thought to make easier for tired feet by the provision of a train ride which could be enjoyed for a small contribution to the funds. Another part of Roland's marketing strategy, of which he was proud, was the sale of Kodak film at lower prices than anywhere else in New York State. He claimed that his best advertisers were satisfied families returning home from their visit and showing friends and neighbours happy snaps. He also told me that in planning additions to the park he always bore in mind the fact that for every extra ten minutes visitors spent at Catskill they were likely to spend an additional 8 cents. I must have raised an eyebrow at some of the commercialism because, reading my thoughts, Roland said on that first visit: 'You may not like some aspects of our operation, but without them we could not have those other parts that you like so much.'

The five-hour journey back to Boston must have been a trial for Walter, for I know I never stopped talking. With a few hazy ideas beginning to buzz around in my head, I somehow knew that this had been an important day. During the course of later visits, sadly without Walter, I realised that in a non-urban setting and with practical but simple buildings, an animal collection of real worth could be established without the vast capital outlays that had created those great zoos of the world which I had come to regard with such awe. On my many subsequent visits to Catskill I was welcomed as a house guest. This too was a treat for a world-weary traveller. The Lindemanns lived in a palatial house close to the Game Farm where dining and wining were in the best traditions of German hospitality, and where in luxurious guest bedrooms my feet would disappear into the deep carpet pile. Early mornings I joined Roland and senior staff members for the daily inspection of the animals, after which we enjoyed cooking and consuming a hearty breakfast in one of Catskill's refreshment kiosks.

The ill-fated Anglo-American Cobb business marriage was terminated after protracted negotiations. The reason was that the original British half of the marriage was then much more profitable than the American half and this did not appear likely to change in the immediate future. The Americans offered Peter Beck and myself (as the two equal owners of the British half) a substantial capital sum each if we would agree to make the union permanent. This had some interest for me. A large farm adjacent to mine in Essex was about to come on the market, and with the sum on offer I could probably have made a purchase which would have made my traditional farming venture more viable and still left me occupying a remunerative post in the poultry industry. With an agreement to make the merger permanent, a celebratory dinner in Concord Massachusetts was enjoyed by the delegations representing both parties. This however was premature, as long before breakfast the next day I was awakened for an anxious discussion with my British colleagues who had slept badly and wished to renege on the agreements of the day before. Whilst to do this was not an honourable act, it was clear that to go further forward with so many misgivings would be disastrous, and so the British chairman and the finance director went to visit Messrs Cobb senior and junior with the news, and everyone but me went home. I was still heavily involved in the American operation and so, with the agreement of both parties, continued a dual role for some years. Both parties were also contractually bound to work together in marketing the Cobb bird for their mutual survival.

I have often wondered since how my life might have gone without that early-morning reversal of an agreement. Ironically, my original farm and the one that I might have bought are now covered in housing. Much later when I had my zoo up and running but facing a financial crisis, I had sold Cut Hedge Farm at an agricultural price and so completely missed all the profits that flow from the fortunes generated by the planning lottery. I have no regrets.

After the demerger the companies owned by Peter Beck and me became subsidiaries of a new holding company named the Anglian Food Group which later became a publicly owned company, and the sale of a portion of my shares was sufficient for me to begin serious thoughts of starting a zoo. Still in a thinking mode, I set off once more for the United States, partly for some Cobb business and partly to make two zoological visits which seemed important to my evolving philosophy, as indeed they proved to be. The first of these was to Phoenix in Arizona where the world herd of Arabian oryx had been established in a last-ditch attempt to save the species. In this it was successful, but we now know (and Roland Lindemann could then have told those involved) that a desert species does not necessarily need a desert environment in which to thrive and reproduce. After a frustrating series of male births this herd became a significant success and a lesson in how zoos can contribute to the saving of a species.

The second Arizona visit was to the Arizona Sonora Desert Museum which was, and is, an outstanding mixture of zoo, botanical garden and environmental park. In fact it is a true theme park (how I dislike the current abuse of that term) with water being the theme, demonstrating its use by specially evolved animals and plants of the Sonora Desert as its underlying *raison d'être*. The impact of the philosophy of this place on me was enormous, and became still more so on a later visit. The underlying thought processes are applicable to the ecology of any region of our planet.

This being summer holiday time I brought my two sons, Christopher and Simon, with me. We began in Boston where I had some business to conduct, after which I hoped that they might meet Walter Stone and his wife Betty and their nine children, some of whom were of comparable ages to my boys. Phone calls elicited the sparse information that Walter was on leave, possibly somewhere on Cape Cod, then as now famous as a retreat of Kennedys and Bushes as well as more ordinary mortals. Not really expecting that we would bump into the Stones in a quite extensive resort, we nevertheless set off to see the famous Cape anyway. There then occurred one of those weird chance happenings that defy rational explanation. We were just drifting with no real purpose when we came to a crossroads. I stopped the car and after a little debate between the three of us Simon said: 'Go straight across.' We did, and within minutes were on a beach with the entire Stone family. A few more minutes saw the youngsters interacting as though they had known each other all their lives.

I did not know it then, but this was to be the last time that I would see Walter alive. He was in a distressed state. His difficulties with the MDC had increased rapidly, and just before his escape to the Cape his keys were taken from him, a pretty sure sign that his career in Boston and possibly in zoos at any senior level was coming to an end. We talked well into the night and early morning. I hope I offered some cheer and comfort. It was just some three weeks later, when I was at a meeting in La Rochelle in France, that I received a message from Fred Zeehandelaar in his office in New Rochelle, New York to tell me that Walter had been killed together with another driver in a head-on car crash in New Hampshire. The funeral date was already set, and I had just time enough to fly to Paris and then London to catch TWA flights to Boston via New York, where the airline lost my luggage so that, for the first and only time in my life I attended a funeral in 'brown boots'.

To my everlasting gratitude Fred Zeehandelaar met me outside the funeral home, where a wake was in progress ahead of the service in Boston's Catholic Cathedral, to prepare me for the American way of death, with an open coffin which I had to approach and then say a prayer. With awful feelings I did this, and there saw Walter repaired from his injuries, looking as I had known him, and wearing a Dublin Zoo tie with giraffe motifs that I had given to him some long while before because he had liked it so much. In the hypocritical way that we humans often conduct our lives and deal with death, the long cathedral service included words of praise for the deceased by some who had hastened his decline and fall. Later, the zoo at Stoneham, the design of which Walter so criticised, was renamed the Walter D. Stone Memorial Zoo.

I was much saddened at the premature end of an all too short but close personal friendship which also had such influence on my future life. I felt deep concern for his widow Betty and the children, all of whom had also become my friends. I have never been particularly good with children but the Stone brood took to me to their hearts and I had become 'Uncle John' early in our acquaintance. Amazingly, two of the boys chose to ride with me in my rented car to the cathedral service. Happily I was later able to help some of the family by treating three of the boys to a European trip and later Betty and two of the girls to a visit to Marwell.

By this time, utterly determined to start a zoo myself, I settled down to plan how this might be accomplished, sadly without my mentor.

Chapter 4

The first decision I had to make was where to situate this zoo that was taking shape in my head. For a number of reasons it had to be in Britain. Almost anywhere else in the developed world, as it then was in the late 1960s, would have presented enormous difficulties caused by currency restrictions. Because my capital and income were both in Britain, that part of the decision was, in modern parlance, a no-brainer! In addition, every cricket season reminds me that although I am very much a citizen of the world, I am capable of being passionately English!

The next decision was: where in Britain? The country was already well covered by wildlife attractions of various sizes and merits, so wherever I chose to seek a site I would find established animal attractions competing for public support – until of course the unique merits of what I planned were widely recognised! Southern England seemed to have some room for what I was planning and also had the benefit of a slightly milder climate than elsewhere. Besides this dubious logic, there was the fact that, although I had lived and been based in Essex all my life, I had a distinct emotional preference for the south. So the search for a property was begun in the general areas of Hampshire, Wiltshire and Dorset. To help with the search I recruited land agent Jim Benham. Jim had helped me with all my property interests for many years, beginning when he assisted my early farming efforts by obtaining a grant for the installation of a sheep dipping complex. As the relationship had grown, I came to appreciate Jim's total integrity and the fact that his sometimes pessimistic view of whatever project was in hand was a much-needed counterbalance to my impulsiveness. Such qualities were to prove invaluable in the years to come.

Our first site visit was to some 600 acres near Salisbury in Wiltshire which once had an obscure wartime use. It was rather flat and boring in appearance with only a few small buildings and young trees decorating lank grass, so a great deal of landscaping would have been needed to make it pleasant for man and beast. It was, however, incredibly cheap and we left it with exciting thoughts of having to spend less than expected on land purchase, therefore leaving a balance for really dramatic earthworks and creative buildings. That hope was short-lived as we were soon warned that some 34 people had rights to graze sheep over the property and those rights had only recently been defended in Britain's highest court, the House of Lords. Sheep all over the place would not work well in a major zoo!

Our next viewing was the unexpected lucky one. The Marwell Hall estate, six miles south-east of Winchester in Hampshire, of some 414 acres, came onto the market in early 1969 at a time when farms were much less sought after than they were soon to become. The truism that 'they stopped making land a long while ago' had yet to be fully appreciated. The property had been acquired by a Mr Bullen some five years previously, with wealth obtained by selling his business which, amongst other things, rented furniture to stand-holders and others at big national shows held at London's Olympia and Earl's Court venues. My company had been such a hirer. Mr Bullen's plan was for the central 100 acres to be a thoroughbred horse-breeding establishment and a fine stable square was built for this purpose. Sadly for him, premature death precluded the fruition of his plans.

Marwell met most of the desirable criteria for the planned zoo. It was well furnished with mature trees, had some fairly free-draining paddocks (important for hoofed animals) and was undulating enough to be visually interesting without being too challenging for pedestrians. It was close to the populations of Portsmouth, Southampton and Winchester with the eventual hope of good road links to south London. It would be from these urban areas that the hoped-for visitors would come, bearing the currency which would support the enterprise. It would have been a bonus had there been water, either a stream or large ponds, for being on a chalk subsoil the construction of water features, as we were to discover, would be both costly and difficult. The disadvantage (and there would be at least one anywhere) was the large edifice of Marwell Hall right in the middle of the planned stud farm's 100 acres, which was the natural area for a zoo. Too big for anything other than gracious living by a wealthy person who did not plan to spend what wealth he had on a zoo, yet not large enough to provide the additional attraction of a stately home, it was then and ever after a source of worry tinged with affection.

On balance, the positives were greater than the negatives so Jim, acting for me, began negotiations with a Mr Cox of Fox & Sons, the agents acting for the vendors. These were protracted and were in progress during my next working visit to the United States. I followed this with a trip to Florida, the objective of which was the compound of Robert Baudy, a circus trainer of big cats, who was also a breeder of Siberian tigers and other wild felines. Robert himself was away with a circus but I was met by his wife, a very gracious lady who had an amazingly attractive little cat at her feet which turned out to be a small South American species called a Kodkod. This was the only time that I have ever seen one of these charming animals.

Mrs Baudy told me that they had just one pair of Siberian tigers for sale – a two-year-old hand-reared half-brother and sister, whose parents were in her husband's current circus act, but who were registered with the studbook keeper (the director of Leipzig Zoo) and thus recognised as pure Siberians. Invited to meet them, I was more than a little taken aback when their cage door was opened and I was ushered into the presence of Boris and Lena. Their greeting was just like that of domestic cats with slightly arched backs, much rubbing against my legs, and with a blowing of air from the mouth, which was a friendly tiger greeting that I was destined to get to know well in the years to come.

I was bowled over by these two in more senses than one and with total recklessness bought them for the then not insubstantial sum of US$10,000. Back in a motel, I had time for reflection and reality struck. In one short afternoon I had committed myself to a zoo-owning future. I telephoned Jim Benham who, although by now well used to my strange ways, was nevertheless surprised at the news of my purchase and the consequent instruction to close the deal to purchase the Marwell Hall estate. This was completed by the signing of an agreement a few days after my return, at a price which would give the vendors an extra

£20,000 if and when we obtained planning permission to establish a zoological park. Completion was to be in early autumn, seven days before my 40th birthday.

Continuing my journey through Florida I was given a surprising insight into a less than attractive aspect of American animal keeping. Travelling along a back road I saw a sign advertising 'Noell's Ark & Alligator Farm'. The similarity to my own surname intrigued me. One of Roland Lindemann's pieces of advice that I have always followed, often to my benefit, was to look at every animal attraction that I came across, no matter how unlikely looking, as there was always the chance that there would be something of interest within. So into Noell's establishment I went where, after explaining my zoo plans and the similarity of surname, I was warmly welcomed, and invited into Mr and Mrs Noell's capacious trailer where they were rearing a baby Orang-utan with all the tender care that a human child would receive. As business seemed less than brisk, I enquired as to their visitor attendances and, by implication, their finances. With great candour I was told that the Florida site was just their winter quarters where they might sometimes hope to make an extra buck from a wandering tourist, but that their real income was derived from travelling the country to state fairs and similar shows, with a sideshow advertising a reward for any strong man who could survive in their boxing ring with one of their 'man-apes'. I was then taken to see a large trailer with a double deck of some dozen tiny cages, each containing an adult Chimpanzee. It was explained that each animal would be muzzled and boxing-type gloves placed on their hands before they were led into the ring to meet a challenger, usually a local tough guy who felt that he could handle 'any monkey'. Seldom was the prize handed out! The muzzle and gloves were to protect the challenger, not the Chimpanzee.

I asked how it was possible to get the muzzle and gloves on these strong animals. The answer was that they were so bored in their tiny cages that they willingly assented to the pre-fight procedures. Commenting that Mr Noell had lost an index finger, I was assured that he still had it and he produced it in a small leather pouch whilst pointing to the largest chimp and saying that he was the culprit. I left depressed that such exploitation of animals was allowed in a modern society, but also perplexed by the contradictory nature of these animal people's attitudes to their charges. During the subsequent years of my involvement with animals and animal people, I was destined to meet with much similar ambivalence.

Back in Britain I had much to do with my demanding 'day job' with the Anglian food group which involved a fairly heavy travel schedule which sometimes, if I was lucky, fitted in with the two matters then dominant in my mind. These were obtaining planning permission for my hoped-for 'Marwell Zoological Park' and acquiring the very special animals which were to distinguish Marwell from its many fellow zoos. The two issues had to be tackled simultaneously because in those days quarantine for the ruminants which were to be such a feature of this brave new zoo was virtually impossible, though I was then cockily sure that for me nothing would be impossible. Reality struck early on, however, because my first purchases, the beautiful tigers from Florida, had to undergo rabies quarantine in a zoo and, to my surprise, no British zoo stepped forward to house and exhibit these animals even though they were dramatically larger and more important, from a conservation standpoint, than the subspecific hybrids then gracing most carnivore exhibits. Although I was acquainted with many zoo people in America, I had the great disadvantage of neither knowing any future colleagues in Britain nor being known by them.

Again I was to have a slice of good fortune. I had heard of the Federation of British Zoos whose Secretary, Geoffrey Schomberg, had an office in London Zoo. On the off-chance of gaining some useful knowledge, I made an appointment to meet this man who, although he had never worked in a zoo, had studied them all his life and had recently written a book about British zoos. I was in luck, for once more I clicked with Geoffrey, and shortly afterwards he came to visit Marwell, where he endorsed my enthusiasm for the site and drew up a rough layout plan which remains the basic road structure to this day. Of immediate importance was Geoffrey's endorsement of myself as a serious and knowledgeable future zoo owner, making introductions which eased my entry into a rather charmed – and often charming – circle of people. He was also destined to be of vital help in the forthcoming planning struggle. Much later he told a mutual friend that during the time of his secretaryship of the Zoo Federation he was contacted by many would-be zoo people but I was the only one that he felt was likely to succeed.

An Old Etonian, Geoffrey always exhibited an air of diffidence which I have sometimes encountered amongst former pupils of that world-famous institution. I have also met others who were assertive often to the point of rudeness. He must have been born into a degree of wealth as apart from his poorly paid post with the Zoo Federation and a second book which was a Penguin publication (also on British zoos) he never appeared to be earning money, and certainly never asked me for any for his help. Much married, his wonderful dry sense of humour made him a delightful companion. I well remember how much quiet pleasure he got from riding in a lift with me after a star-studded fundraising party for the Federation sponsored by Martini Rossi and telling me later that we had shared this ride with two of his ex-wives. Sadly, a long sojourn in France and a premature death prevented him from witnessing Marwell's eventual blossoming.

Through Geoffrey's intervention, Cyril Grace, who was then the director of Dudley Zoo, agreed to quarantine Boris and Lena at a satellite zoo in Birmingham. I was to pay for the adaptation of a cage and the costs of their keep whilst they were there. It was a very good deal for this small zoo as these enormous tigers were a good attraction throughout a full visitor season.

Once it was decided that I would purchase the Marwell Hall estate, Jim and I began the planning process, firstly with some informal chats with planning officers, most of whom were, to say the least, discouraging. An early reaction was that any application would be premature as the long-term plan for South Hampshire was still 'work in progress'. Moreover, proposals to link Portsmouth and Southampton, incorporating all the built-up areas in between, thus creating 'Solent City', would have such an impact on the whole infrastructure of the area that no major projects could go forward until all these considerations were resolved. One other bizarre reason put forward for delay was that the Marwell site and its immediate surrounds were being considered, among others, for a third London airport!

In the tradition of all good bureaucrats, the planners favoured 'masterly inactivity'. Such was not my way of doing things, and because it was eventually to be a County Council decision, we made

48

a formal outline planning application in May 1970 that then went to all levels of local government for discussion and opinion in the true spirit of democracy. The first of these public participation exercises was held, on a very hot June evening, in the village hall of Owslebury, the parish in which Marwell lies. Until that very hot June day I had always thought that any neighbourhood would be thrilled to have a zoo in its midst at no cost to itself. How naive I was! My first hint of the hostility that I was to face came when I phoned the titled lady whose land adjoined Marwell. After introducing myself, I asked if I might call on her and tell her of my plans. For half an hour I listened to a non-stop tirade of abuse down the phone line, which was the forerunner of an evening in which Jim and I were the recipients of verbal venom such as neither of us had ever experienced. Being eaten in your bed by tigers was certain to stem from Knowles's scheme to make himself rich, as was the inevitable cessation of milk production by cows in the area, together with the impossibility of harvesting crops because of the lanes being blocked by cars and 'charabancs'. These were just a few of the fears expressed and hurled at us with amazing venom.

> In the summer of '69
> There came to us a man
> He had bought our local Marwell Hall –
> And put to us a plan.

> "Aha! I plan to turn this place
> Into a wild life Zoo,
> With snow leopards, and wolves, and bears,
> And white rhinos too."

> So did he say – and little knew
> The furore he had started
> For some were for – and some against
> Owslebury in two was parted.

> We nattered in our homes and streets
> We argued in the pubs.
> Our natters grew to a great big roar,
> Like a – leopard with its cubs!

"Let's call a meeting in the Hall,
Conflict will never cease
Till we confront this Mr Knowles
The villain of the piece."

"Traffic and coaches through our lanes?
Begone the very thought."
The pen is mightier than the sword –
And by golly how we fought –

The local paper was beseiged
With letters by the ream
And some said "No" and some said "YES"
They liked the Knowles man's dream.

Interviews on the TV
Reporters' pens a-flying
It seems that this has killed the myth
That Owslebury is dying!

(The lady ghost in Marwell Hall
She wrings her hands in dread,
"This man should live in Henry's time,
He'd surely lose his head.")

Petitions came, petitions went,
We signed our names to one,
And now sit back, and watch and wait
To see what will be done.

And so – if tigers come our way,
Wolves, rhinos, bears from the poles,
We'll have to learn to live with them.
With them – and MR KNOWLES!

D.E.F., an Owslebury resident

A few brave villagers later emerged as very valuable allies in the months to come, but that night showed me just how fierce passions can be stirred and how a large crowd becomes dangerous. Tales of lynch mobs passed through my mind! At other similar public meetings we encountered more opposition than support but they were always of a more reasonable and civilised nature. The letter columns of the local papers were filled with opinions for and against my plans, many of both being ill-informed but passionate. Local radio and television also enjoyed the controversy but the media then, as in subsequent years, were generally supportive.

Earlier in the day of the bruising experience in Owslebury, I made a courtesy call on Jimmy Chipperfield whose growing animal empire included a rather indifferent zoo on Southampton Common, which was his very first venture outside circus and therefore had a warm place in his affections. It was obvious that if my plans came to fruition they would have a negative impact on this. Jimmy was however most gracious, saying that Britain was a free country in which we could all follow our wishes if they were lawful. Secretly, he probably thought that I was a bumbling amateur unlikely to succeed.

Jimmy was a member of a famous circus family which in the post-war era had operated one of the three big tenting shows travelling in Britain. Having broken away from the family business he had a varied career dealing in hay and straw and promoting horse shows before starting two small zoos (the other one was in Plymouth) and then developing the 'drive-through' animal park concept firstly at Longleat and then worldwide. He was a man of great determination and his early story is best told in a remarkable book by the artist Edward Seago called *High Endeavour* which tells of how, with no previous formal schooling, he set about correcting this in order to qualify as an RAF pilot in World War II. To me he was ever friendly and gracious, although I suspected that his early frequent visits to Marwell might have been in the hope that it would fail and could be acquired advantageously.

With the planning furore at its height, I completed the purchase of the estate. Because the majority of the land was being farmed it had been agreed that this should be done on the traditional Michelmas Day, so I duly lodged the necessary money with my Norwich-based solicitors ready for transfer on 29th September. On that day I was working in my office in Essex when I received a worried phone call from the vendor's solicitors asking why we had not completed. My call to the Norfolk partner dealing with this elicited the information that he expected to complete on old Michelmas Day which in his area was still 11th October. The change of the Michelmas date had occurred a mere hundred or so years before!

As so often happens with property exchanges, relations between seller and purchaser were often fraught. It began with my refusal to buy the contents of Marwell Hall in one lot, which was a mistake on my part as at a subsequent auction sale it was quite clear that I could have cleared a handsome profit, but my priorities were not expensive furniture and fittings. My subsequent refusal to purchase a large pile of coal for which I had no possible use further darkened my character. Hampshire County Council and Winchester City Council decided to support my planning application but very unfortunately the Owslebury elite had the ear of Winchester's then Conservative Member of Parliament. He used his influence to have the application 'called in' which meant a full public enquiry conducted by an inspector appointed by a Secretary of State who would eventually make a decision based on the inspector's report. The two-week enquiry held in the Hampshire County Council's headquarters was a fairly brutal affair with barristers representing two different groups of objectors and a barrister representing myself instructed by my solicitors. The County Council had one of its own solicitors supporting our cause.

Of the two opponents, one represented the residents of Twyford, a village through which many of Marwell's visitors were likely to drive. Twyford had then, and still has, a traffic problem with a sharp bend on a very narrow main street. They really wanted not to stop the zoo, but to get a bypass for the village. Many villagers have since contacted me apologising for their objection, and indicating genuine appreciation of the zoological park. The barrister for the Owslebury group was determined to conduct the whole affair as though it was a major criminal trial. Although witnesses in planning enquiries are not on oath they are expected to tell the truth, which during nearly two days of cross-examination by this man, I did. I shall never, however, forget his very meaningful sniffs whenever an answer of mine was not what he wanted, followed by the loaded expression: 'I hear what you say.'

When this ordeal (for such it was) was over I had to consider the likely outcome and the options that a decision either way would offer. Generally my team was optimistic. Jim quite rightly insisted that the farming of the land that was not scheduled for the zoo and the estate generally should be managed so that in the event of failure some losses could be recouped by a sale. For my part I worried that the large cost of the enquiry coupled with the ensuing delay, at a time of high inflation, was eating away at the available capital. This meant that I must have animals available and building plans drawn up for their housing so that there should be as little time lost as possible between receiving the planning permission and an opening which would trigger a cash inflow.

The time between the planning enquiry and its resolution was a difficult one, but unwisely in the view of many (and logically I have to say they were right) further animal acquisitions began during that period. By a joyous Saturday 22nd May 1971, when the Southampton *Daily Echo* phoned to say that we had won the day, a number of animals were already with us at Marwell and others were undergoing quarantine or were being held in, by then, co-operative zoos. Before the good news arrived, we had provided as much animal accommodation as we could without seriously infringing planning regulations. The fine stable yard created by the late Mr Bullen was the early centre for animal arrivals, the first of which, fittingly, were Boris and Lena, whilst elsewhere in the complex zebras were housed in buildings designed for their domesticated cousins. With money by then haemorrhaging at a frightening rate it was necessary to open to the public and begin some cash inflow as soon as possible. An opening date of 22nd May 1972 was set. This was one of my biggest mistakes; one which came close to destroying all my long-cherished plans and dreams . . .

Chapter 5

The last 30 years of the 20th century brought changes into the world of zoos as great as or greater than those that affected every aspect of life on Planet Earth. Most important amongst these have been the achievements stemming from improved biological knowledge and the consequent successes of breeding in zoos. Only in very rare instances is it now necessary for animals to be captured from the wild. Collectively, zoos have a goal of, at the very least, maintaining self-sustaining populations. With mammals, these successes have been of such a magnitude that birth control is often necessary. Before deploring the original capture of wild animals for zoos, it should be remembered that without these some species would be extinct and many more in danger of becoming so. The vast trade in wild species for the pet trade is another matter altogether and is to be deplored both for its impact on endemic populations and its cruelty.

In the 21st century, movements of animals between responsible zoos are largely governed by studbook managers and species coordinators, who are usually zoo staff undertaking these responsibilities in addition to their full-time work. Supported by committee structures, these people recommend exchanges between zoos based on genetics and perceived management capabilities. It is still necessary for participating zoos to obtain permits to conform to conservation legislation and to meet national and international veterinary regulations. These latter are now less stringent than when Marwell was assembling its inhabitants, because government veterinary authorities have come to recognise that zoos are responsible institutions which can be trusted, at least as much as the agricultural community, in matters affecting national animal health.

When I was assembling Marwell's founding populations, all animals had a monetary value and were exchanged sometimes directly between zoos, often for cash, but most often through animal dealers. Because Marwell was new it had no animals for sale or exchange so the major early acquisitions were made through animal dealers who, I must say, generally served me well. It is to their credit that as the sale and purchase of animals became a thing of the past most dealers applied their expertise to the formidable tasks of arranging shipping and dealing with the reams of paperwork that any animal movement generates.

The zoo world has a very effective bush telegraph and shortly after my plans became public I was contacted by Mrs Lettie Vantol, then acting as the British agent for her Dutch brother-in-law, Frans van den Brink, one of the major European wild animal dealers specialising in mammals. Although, necessarily, profit-driven, Frans was pleased to find in me someone whose main interest was in hoofed animals. He had himself been responsible for the catching of two semi-desert African species, both of which were destined to face near-extinction in the wild within decades, and both of which are now secure in captive populations. These are the Scimitar-horned oryx and the Dama gazelle. The Scimitars were placed by Frans in certain zoos which had been able to receive the initial wild-caught animals. The offspring of these animals were then distributed to zoos in Europe and America, often under complex agreements which ensured future profits for Frans. Early in our business relationship, Frans encouraged me to visit Aalborg Zoo in Denmark which was his European holding zoo for Scimitar-horned oryx. It was there that, once again, I fell in love with a species of stunning physical beauty and grace of movement and immediately decided that not only should some of these come to Marwell, but that the species should become the symbol of the zoo's purpose.

My decision, however, had formidable obstacles in its way in the shape of almost impossible veterinary regulations that were concerned with maintaining the disease control benefits bestowed on by Britain by its island status. Foot and mouth disease was the primary source of anxiety. Exotic ruminant imports were required to spend 12 months in an urban environment which was then defined as a place where there were no domestic cattle, sheep or goats within a 1-mile radius. One might at first think that it should not have been difficult to find such a place in crowded England. However, this is not in practice the case, because small fingers of farmland jut into most built-up areas. It is hard, however, to escape the conclusion that the senior bureaucrats in the government veterinary department of those days saw these conditions as a way of avoiding the irritation of the likely import of a few zoo animals. Such difficulties had not always been in place, as there was a small number of cloven-hoofed exotic species already in British zoos.

With great energy and determination, Frans, a man after my own heart, arranged to hire a warehouse in that part of Greater Manchester then famous for the television soap opera *Coronation Street*, in which the first month of very close quarantine could take place. The animals would then be moved to Manchester's Bellevue, a large entertainment complex owned in those days by the Trust House Forte catering and hotel group, which had a large zoo at its centre. As with the very first tigers in Birmingham, Bellevue Zoo (which was then already in decline and destined to close in 1977) was more than happy to have animal 'stars' to entice visitors with the additional benefit of their owners paying for their board and lodging to boot!

Into this first quarantine came the largest consignment of exotic hoofed animals to enter the UK for many years. In addition to my nucleus herd of Scimitar-horned oryx we added groups of Ellipsen waterbuck and Nyala which, like the Scimitars, have descendants still flourishing at Marwell. A group of Impala, one of Africa's most common antelopes, was included. This was a mistake on my part, not just because of their abundance in the wild, but because of their extreme nervousness. Impala demonstrate acute flight behaviour, which is a necessary survival strategy for animals destined to be a main course for Africa's larger carnivores. They did not thrive at Marwell, ironically because we gave them space which awakened all their flight behaviour instincts, leading to fatal collisions with chainlink fencing. Surrounded by the solid walls of the urban zoo they had remained calm. Also there was a trio of White-tailed wildebeest (then considered potentially endangered) which were with us for a long time with no offspring. We later found the male's semen to be less than viable. There was also a pair of Goral, animals which are from an intriguing family known as goat antelopes, which also failed to breed. This was just as well as they were eventually proven to be from parents of different branches of the same family and therefore subspecific hybrids. Purity of species and subspecies is always the goal of a conscientious breeder of wild animals, with cross-breeding only to be tolerated when a population is without hope of continuing without such a crossing.

One of the business strengths of Frans was his ability to deal behind the Iron Curtain, which for so long dominated every aspect of life in Europe after World War II. Like all Dutchmen he was proficient in many languages, and possessed of great self-confidence. Frans sold us our first six Giraffe which came from a small town called Dvur Kralove in Czechoslovakia – from an amazing zoo which the Communist Party had allowed to acquire from African countries and hold (as it does today) Europe's largest collection of animals from that continent. I believe that its founder, Josef Wagner, was a high-ranking Communist and thus had freedoms denied to most other zoos behind the Iron Curtain. I have had several opportunities to visit this zoo over the years and the visits have always been mind-blowing, both as to the numbers of species and the numbers of individuals within those species. The zoo's successful animal management during the harsh winters of Central Europe is amazing. The Ministry of Agriculture must have succumbed to van den Brink's persuasiveness for the Giraffe were allowed to go straight to their 12 months' quarantine in Bellevue. No way could they have been housed in the low warehouse in the environment of *Coronation Street* that had served as the first taste of Britain for the smaller animals.

Movement of animals is always traumatic both for them and for the human carers involved, although I have often noticed that after a few early complaints animals settle into new homes much more quickly than people. The arrival of the Scimitars was an unnecessarily bloody business. The then Director of Aalborg Zoo, who should have known better, placed each individual in a crate with long slats as the roof, through which three of the animals had thrust their long graceful horns, panicked and snapped off large lengths. Antelope horns, like those of cows, are filled with blood vessels and because of their position, if broken, the blood is very hard to staunch. This was accomplished without loss of life, but as antelope and cattle horns, unlike a deer's antlers, do not regrow, we had two animals with bent and unsightly horns and one with none. Amazingly No Horns, as this last animal became known, never appeared to be aware of her loss and was always amongst the most dominant of the females.

Footpaths and bridleways enabled the local population to keep an eye on all that was happening in our future zoo. One amusing comment that found its way back to me was: 'That fellow Knowles may know something about tigers and suchlike, but he certainly doesn't know anything about horses. You should see the useless animals that someone has stuck him with.' Little did they know that those 'useless horses' were at that time amongst the world's rarest mammal species. They were Przewalski's wild horses, which are physically distinguished from domestic horses by their short backs and rather upright pasterns, which would certainly make them an uncomfortable ride – which explains the judgement of our horse-wise neighbours. They also have tails that are thin at the base, rather upright manes and zebra-like markings on their legs. They have noses that look as though they have bran meal stuck to them, a feature which they share with Britain's Exmoor ponies (thought by many authorities to be the last descendants of Europe's extinct wild ponies). Most significantly, they are also distinguished from all other horses by having two more chromosomes.

I had first fallen in love with these animals during one of my weekends at Catskill when, as a 'thank you' for the hospitality which I was receiving, I cleaned out the yard of the off-exhibit herd. The horses were discovered towards the end of the 19th century by Colonel Przewalski, a count in the employ of the Czar of Russia, who shot an animal from whose skin the species was identified and named after him, with the addition of the name of Poliakoff, the scientist in Saint Petersburg Museum who recognised the new species, so that the full scientific name of the horse is *Equus przewalskii poliakoff* (1881). Later a few animals were captured and offspring from a small founder population became established in zoos in Europe. In Britain the Duke of Bedford's Woburn Park had the largest herd.

The last sighting of the species in the wild was in 1963 in a remote part of Mongolia and by 1970 they were regarded as extinct in the wild. A studbook had been established which was kept at Prague Zoo where the first of a number of meetings was held at which interested parties committed themselves to the preservation of this unique animal.

In 1980 Marwell was proud to host one of these meetings, amongst the delegates to which were members of the Mongolian Embassy staff in London, demonstrating a belated interest in *their* horses. From this began a dialogue which was eventually to take me on two exciting journeys to that country.

In the days when I wished to form a herd of Przewalski's as part of Marwell's commitment to endangered species, I came upon two difficulties. The first of these was that few breeders had significant numbers of animals and therefore most had few if any to spare. The second was that most breeders (and the many interested fans of the species) recognised two bloodlines. One was the so-called Prague line which was almost certainly corrupted by the genes of a domestic mare at the time of the first captures, but which was less subject to inherited problems such as ataxia, and more prolific than the less obviously corrupted Munich line. Most of the Prague line animals carried manes that were less than upright and had colour variations that were regarded as undesirable evidence of the unfortunate early misalliance. The Munich line animals were generally closer to the perceived desirable appearance. The 'type specimen' is the animal shot by the gallant Colonel, identified and mounted in the Hermitage Museum in St Petersburg.

To complicate the situation further, Prague Zoo had the benefit of a known pure stallion called Bars, whose mother, Orlica 3, was the last animal to be taken from the wild in 1947. She was kept in the Soviet animal breeding centre, Askania Nova in the Ukraine, where unbelievably she was first bred to domestic horses. However Bars, her only pure offspring, was transferred to Prague Zoo where his genetic influence was of great importance. By another of my strokes of good fortune, Russian troops had fired some shots into the Prague Zoo at the time of the Dubcek rising in Czechoslovakia and the Director, Professor Zdenek Vesselosky, a fine man who was later to lose his post to a Communist nominee, decided that his herd should be reduced in number and animals became available to breeders in the West. These were offered through Frans van den Brink, from whom I purchased some mares of the old line and – very importantly for my plans for the species – two young females who were daughters of Bars.

To reach my goal of achieving the very best genetic make-up in the Marwell herd, I needed a stallion of the Munich line. Catskill's herd was entirely derived from Munich animals, but a young pair purchased earlier from there had been an early disappointment. The male died in transit and the female lingered with us for a long time suffering from ataxia and eventually had to be euthanased on humanitarian grounds. Out of the blue I received a telex (the most efficient form of communication before fax and e-mails) from Fred Zeehandelaar, offering an adult stallion of the Munich–Catskill line named Catskill Basil. For reasons that have never been clear to me, Basil was then in the ownership of a dentist in Ohio who had intended to establish a collection of wild equids, but never accomplished it.

Fred was one of the many great characters on the edge of the zoo world. His charm was his rudeness; endless sniffs marked his forthright expressions of opinion which usually ran contrary to those with whom he was doing business. He was scrupulously honest and very efficient, and consequently respected in his field. Born in Holland, he crossed to Britain in a small boat in 1940 and served in the British Army. At war's end he saw little prospect for himself in Europe and emigrated to America, where he found employment in a New York shipping office. One consignment for which he was responsible at that time was a group of wild-caught zebras. Spotting a profitable niche, he struck out on his own and established a business as an importer and dealer in wild animals, from which he never looked back

From my office in Essex, I negotiated with Fred about Basil by looking over the shoulders of a secretary who typed my side of the discussion into the telex machine. Having nearly reached a mutually agreeable price, I asked, as a last bargaining ploy, if Fred would guarantee that Basil was capable of breeding, for he had been on his own for a long time. I could imagine the sniffs as back came the answer: 'My name is Zeehandelaar . . . not God'! Basil came to us and was the very successful sire of many foals, and my strategy of breeding from what were in effect three lines of Przewalski's wild horse was a great success. When his daughters reached breeding age it was time for Basil to move on. His presence was then requested by San Diego Zoo, where he also sired many offspring and where I saw him once more, before old age overtook him, enjoying retirement in a warmer climate than that of Hampshire. Przewalski's wild horses have bred so well at Marwell and elsewhere, including in Mongolia (more of which later), that the species can now be regarded as 'safe'. Marwell and like-minded zoos were crucial to securing the future of the species, and must continue to keep some as an insurance policy and as an educational example of what zoos can do for conservation.

One charismatic species that I wished to have almost more than any other was the Okapi, then as now rare in zoos, and of unknown numerical status in its only home, the vast Ituri forest of the Democratic Republic of Congo. I had been enthralled by this little-known relative of the Giraffe ever since, as a small boy, I read in a magazine that London Zoo had a very rare animal (a mammal not known to science until 1901) which was housed off-exhibit in one end of the long since demolished, but then fabulous, cattle shed. The article said that by pushing a bell and then pressing a shilling into the hand of the keeper who opened the door, this wondrous animal could be viewed. An indulgent uncle obliged and I have been starstruck ever since.

I mentioned this near obsession of mine to van den Brink who amazed me by offering me a male Okapi, then at Basle Zoo, for the staggeringly low price of US$1,500. I took a trip to Basle where I was met at the airport by the famous and ever-courteous Director, Ernst Lang, who showed me some of the their ground-breaking breeding programmes, including Gorillas and Pygmy hippos, both then seldom bred in zoos. Sometimes, like most people who have spent their lives with animals, I have an instinct for trouble and looking at this male Okapi I had distinctly bad vibrations and reluctantly declined the opportunity to fulfil a childhood dream. As it turned out my instincts were right, for van den Brink moved him to his base in Soest in Holland where he died shortly after. Happily, much later when money rather than dedication and expertise had ceased to be the criteria for species acquisition, Marwell became one of the world's major Okapi centres.

Returning to the story of Marwell's progress to a zoo open for paying visitors, I was by the summer of 1971 relieved of the worry of what would I do with the animals already acquired if the zoo was not to happen, but needed to begin building on a large scale. Other than the tigers and the Przewalski's horses, the animals were at various stages of their quarantine periods, most of which would end in a matter of months. Time was not on my side! Fortunately in the interim I had formulated firm ideas as to what types of buildings were wanted and where they should go. But not a single sod had been turned to begin changing the zoo on paper into one with real roads and buildings. To begin with I had to recruit building staff (and needed a first-class foreman to lead a team and manage contractors) and an in-house team. It was urgent that the zoo be ready for an early opening in 1972, for the vitally necessary inflow of cash. I was still committed to the 'day job' and was not able to spend as much time on site as I would have liked, although with the indulgence of my colleagues I did steal far more days than I should.

Jim Benham and I interviewed a number of applicants through a long and trying day, at the end of which we were less than happy with any of the candidates. That evening I received a phone call from a Mrs Lines. She was aware that the deadline for applications was passed but her husband was tired of assembly-line construction work on modern housing estates and would dearly like to be considered for the job. Rather reluctantly I agreed to see him the following day, and thank goodness I did, for once again Dame Fortune chose to smile on me. Les Lines was one of the first of the stalwart people who believed in the ethos that was the foundation of Marwell, and until ill health forced him to take early retirement, his calm thoughtfulness in the face of seemingly endless crises was a much-needed strength. He and I pegged out the roads, wherever possible giving them interesting bends, through the mature trees and around the sites for animal houses and enclosures.

Over the years since opening I have often been congratulated on our landscaping and the variation in contours that are so much a part of Marwell. I always smile at this because the changes of levels, particularly those of the roadway from the entrance, were born of a problem that at first looked large enough to capsize our all too fragile budget. It was simply that to provide foundations for roads and buildings we had to remove very large amounts of topsoil and subsoil. To pay for it to be taken off site would have been prohibitively expensive, so without a word to planners (or to Jim who constantly worried that we might infringe planning or other regulations) we decided on tipping it in such a way as to provide a gently rising roadway to the higher ground in the centre of the Park. I bought a beat-up Dodge tipper truck and, for as many days as possible, had enormous fun as a lorry driver, taking soil dug by a contractor with a crawler tractor equipped with hydraulic arms and a bucket, and depositing it where Les supervised the levelling and consolidation of the base for a roadway that had to be capable of carrying the heavy loads that a zoo's needs create.

All of those first buildings were necessarily simple but were right for their inhabitants. They arrived on site in prefabricated form and were erected by the maker's staff on concrete bases that Les and his team had prepared. Those simple buildings had, as would become apparent when the public were admitted, the disadvantage of no indoor viewing facility for visitors, and because animals sensibly prefer to stay in the warm and out of the rain on those all too frequent British wet and cold weather days, this led to many early complaints.

Based on the very successful way that we had kept our first intake of zebras in the original stable yard, we housed them in individual loose boxes which each animal quickly learnt to have as their own. This avoided a problem which I knew was so often the cause of injury and mortality when zebras are housed together at night. Because they are nervous animals, a sudden noise or flash of light may cause a panic, leading to kicking and biting. Almost from the beginning we had breeding success with the attractive but common Plains zebras of the southern African form and the taller and more elegant Grevy's which are endangered and now only survive in viable numbers in northern Kenya.

In addition to the tigers, the cat family was represented by two pairs of Leopards, a trio of Jaguars, a pair of European lynx and a pair of Clouded leopards. All the big cats had large outside enclosures and inside dens with wooden floors and glass panels that did enable visitors to see the inmates from outside. Tigers like water in warm weather so their enclosures had pools. A successful innovation was to provide the two species of climbing cats, the Leopards and Jaguars, with outside enclosures built around living trees. As this entailed fixing a roof around branches and ensuring its security, this was not an easy task. However, it paid great dividends both for animals and for the knowledgeable visitor. It is wonderful to look up into the branches and see a leopard lying on a branch with all four legs dangling downwards in a classic African pose.

These additional cats served their six-month rabies quarantine at the winter quarters of Chipperfield's Circus. This was necessary because a rabies scare in Surrey had led to the Ministry of Agriculture announcing a forthcoming ban on the import of all rabies-susceptible animals, which would have denied Marwell its planned diversity of species. It was the quick response of Mrs Vantol, the dealer from whom we were buying these animals, which made this arrangement possible. The use of these winter quarters cages achieved our needs but the ambience was depressing for animals and humans. To supervise the quarantine, we were fortunate in having an experienced keeper who volunteered for this rather grim six-month assignment.

Our animal staff had more or less recruited itself in much the same strange way that so much of Marwell's history had unfolded. The Curator of the small zoo in Birmingham where Boris and Lena had served their rabies quarantine was a young man, Stephan Ormerod, who had begun his career in Gerald Durrell's Jersey Zoo, then a pacesetter for conservation within the zoo world. Highly motivated by concerns for conservation and animal welfare, he saw in my plans for Marwell the career niche that he sought and so, after a brief discussion, he came with the tigers and his young family to live at Marwell. As our animal family grew he arranged for two more former Jersey keepers, Richard McLaren and Ian Maddock, to join us and it was Richard who volunteered for the circus winter quarters assignment.

The appointment of a veterinary surgeon who would be an enthusiastic team member was vital. The excellent vet who had supervised the quarantine of Boris and Lena in Birmingham suggested Richard Hartley, a man he had served with in World War II. Richard was delighted to come on board, and although his only previous experience with other than British domestic animals had been selecting camels for that part of the war in the Middle East, he rapidly learnt a great deal about our kind of inhabitants and was a rock until his premature death robbed us of his skill and quiet wisdom.

Inadvertently his faith in Marwell and its young enthusiastic staff was nearly the cause of an incident that might have damaged our chances of obtaining planning consent and dented our professional credibility. Stephan, unknown to Richard Hartley and me, obtained an amount of one of the immobilising drugs that may only be used under the direction of a veterinary surgeon and which are vital to the safe and humane movement of wild animals. With this he had attempted suicide. Sadly, this talented and capable young man was emotionally unstable and when I returned to Marwell from a business trip I was told that he had been found unconscious by a colleague and was in Winchester Hospital. Amazingly, Stephan recovered and no embarrassing enquiries were made as to how he had obtained the means of self-destruction. Inevitably this was the end of his employment at Marwell, and his position was filled by Ian Maddock and Richard McLaren as joint curators, a situation which lasted until a few months after the opening of Marwell to the public. After leaving Marwell, Stephan became one of a small number of failed zoo employees who turn against the institutions that they were once so keen to embrace. Stephan co-authored with a former Chester Zoo vet a virulently anti-zoo book called *The Last Great Wild Beast Show* which sought to damage the very causes that they had once cherished. Many years later I heard that Stephan had eventually succeeded in terminating his own life.

As 1971 rolled on every day saw greater changes to the face of the former stud farm, as roads were established, buildings erected and animals arrived. As I rushed from one business problem somewhere in Europe or America to another, and then back to Marwell for as long a time as possible, I watched these daily changes. Once in a while I was there to deal with an intransigent problem and by throwing my toys out of the pram managed to accomplish such miracles as persuading two utility providers to use the same trench! This was a time when Britain was still sinking under an attitude of 'can't be done', which was in monumental conflict with someone who, if he had learnt nothing else across the Atlantic, had developed a 'can do' philosophy.

A day of drama was the one when our six Giraffe were to come from Manchester. The firm erecting their house had subcontracted the roofing to a specialist firm who failed to turn up on the appointed day, but assured us that they would have the first layer of roofing felt on whilst the animals were travelling down the motorways. The day dawned with strong winds and driving rain which the roofing men then said made it too dangerous for them to work on a high building. They were not risking their lives for Giraffe! Water was dripping through the unclad roof and the three lorries, each with two Giraffe on board, had left Manchester before dawn. No way could these precious animals not be unloaded on their arrival, and no way could they begin life in Hampshire in a leaking building. Les had the answer. If I would go onto the roof with him and we roped ourselves to each other and kept to opposite sides of the ridge, we could fix enough underfelt to make the building temporarily dry. This we did with much help and encouragement from below, including a message from Ian who was travelling with the animals to tell us that the police escort had lost them! Unbelievably all arrived safely and were eating in their new home by midnight.

Gradually, as some buildings were completed and fences built, it was possible to move animals from their temporary homes either at Marwell or elsewhere into permanent accommodation. One tragedy struck at this time as a result of our collective lack of experience. One by one we darted the Grevy's zebras in the stable yard to immobilise them for the short journey to their new complex, where each was placed in its own loose box and the antagonist drug administered to bring them round. All seemed to have gone well, but a few hours later two of the mares were seen to be circling in their box in a dazed fashion, grazing their heads as they brushed against the walls. Richard Hartley who had supervised the moves was puzzled. He phoned David Jones, then the veterinary surgeon at Whipsnade, who advised that sometimes the first drug will continue cycling despite the administration of the antagonist and the solution was simply to repeat the dose of that second drug. Sadly this advice came too late and we lost both females. This was a real body blow as we had assembled a group of this endangered species which had excellent breeding potential.

A little while later I was offered the chance to buy three more females, but the money had run out for such purchases. There and then I decided to sell the last of the 'toys' which I had acquired in my business days, a Rolls-Royce, and use the money for these animals. This was one of my best ever decisions. There was simply no contest as to the relative importance of beautiful animals and an engineered status symbol. The Grevy's herd went on to be one of Marwell's great success stories, with many generations of foals. However, this took longer than I had hoped. With herd animals, breeding requires only one male to a number of females and the excess males, because of their hostility to each other, if females are even anywhere near, are something of a liability. So we usually hope for female offspring with almost every birth. With all but one mammal species, Pygmy hippo, where female offspring predominate, sex ratios at birth are 50–50 but, as when playing heads and tails with a coin, one or the other may prevail for a number of tosses and a large number of tosses is needed to achieve this ratio. Our Grevy's herd started with five male foals in succession!

Happily there were also some light-hearted moments. In our struggle to assemble the animal groups it had been necessary to park some in rather odd places. Frank Farrar of Colchester Zoo had made an odd corner paddock available for the most important of the Przewalski's from Prague Zoo, two daughters and a son of Bars. Ian and I went to collect these with a small cattle float, which we conveniently (so we thought) backed into an apex to the paddock, so that all we had to do was spread some hay and pony nuts on the ramp of the lorry, walk around the animals and gently urge them into the carriage which was to take them to their glorious future. They thought differently, and round and round in this small paddock we circled on what was an exceptionally warm day. In the midst of our struggles Frank showed up to give us some encouragement. Now, although he owned a zoo, it has to be said that his animal knowledge was less than extensive. On this occasion he managed to undo what little we had achieved by throwing bananas at horses that had never seen such a fruit in their lives. Thankfully he left us to our work and eventually Ian and I prevailed and Bars's precious offspring were soon on their way to Hampshire.

So, sometimes exultantly and sometimes almost despairingly, Marwell moved towards 22nd May 1972 and our appointed opening day.

Chapter 6

An opening, whether of something as big and grand as a new terminal at London's Heathrow airport, or as humble as a village fete, is expected to be a grand occasion. It is looked forward to for many months and conducted with much ceremony, when all has been long prepared and every nook and cranny has been smartened to a degree that it may never achieve again. The excitement and anticipation felt by everyone involved is electric and is a strange mixture of pride and anxiety.

Of these emotions I felt only anxiety on 22nd May 1972 as the 10 a.m. opening time approached for, truth to tell, the much publicised Marwell looked more like a recreation of a World War I battlefield than a brave new breed of forward-looking zoo whose role was to conserve species and give pleasurable education to the masses waiting breathlessly to see the wonders within. I approached our entrance to open the gates and welcome the first paying customer in a steady drizzle of the kind that was typical of the first six weeks of Marwell's life as a public attraction. The entrance at that time consisted of two very modest garden-type sheds each with a lift-up shutter cunningly designed so that anyone leaving in a hurry with their tickets and change would bring the heavy shutter down on their head! As I opened the gate and signalled to Tom Murray (our first senior gatekeeper and one of the many heroic figures without whom there would be no story to tell) to be ready for business, I saw a straggling line of some 15 people waiting for admission. Most of these were people who had supported the concept of Marwell from its very early days including, at the head of the queue, a local councillor, the late Sam White, who although living in the parish of Owslebury had bravely supported us from day one and given evidence at the public enquiry where Marwell's future existence was decided. As recognition for this I had given Sam a ticket for life but he was insistent that he wished to purchase the very first admission ticket to keep for posterity.

His first sight once inside the Park's perimeter would probably have been of a yellow earth-moving machine and beyond that, nestling in a little valley which was the first view of Marwell for a visitor, a disreputable-looking marquee which housed an appalling catering concession organised by our first catering manager. He, like so many early staff members, had been attracted to my dream and left the comparative security of being the landlord of a local pub for a life of greater adventure. What was to become Treetops Restaurant, a building that was to serve us for over 30 years, was still a construction site. As Sam and our other early patrons followed the still unpaved road on its winding route, they would have seen, if they were lucky, Giraffe, Nyala, Ellipsen waterbuck, Cheetah, Impala, White-tailed gnu, Blackbuck, Nilgai, Goral, Przewalski's horses, Kulan (wild asses), Grevy's zebras, Hartmann's mountain zebras and the result of the Brothers Heck's breeding programmes, the reconstructed wild horse of Europe, the Tarpan.

The Grevy's zebras and the Scimitar-horned oryx were together, as they are to this day, in the central paddock immediately in front of Marwell Hall. This has always been one of Marwell's finest sights. Prior to opening I had been advised by an authority on captive animal management that mixing two species, both from arid parts of Africa (but without a shared range in modern times) would lead to conflicts. He suggested that I should divide the paddock in two so that the species could be kept separately. In dealing with animals there are no certainties and he may yet prove to be right, but for 30 years each group has ignored the other. Initially the paddock also held beautiful African crowned cranes which had necessarily had their wings pinioned to prevent them flying away, a procedure that has no ill effects on a bird that spends most of its life feeding on the ground. It took three months for the zebras to discover that they could run the cranes down and kill them, so the cranes were quickly rehoused. Ostriches, which also inhabit this paddock, are to the surprise of many more than a match for other animals and are capable of inflicting severe harm to any animal, including the human one, as I can testify from painful experience!

The stable yard, with the rather unattractive utilitarian enclosures which we had added to the original rather grand buildings, was referred to with a certain economy of the truth as the 'acclimatisation area', and was the place to see the most animals. Here at the beginning were the Chapman's zebras and the majority of our wild cats including Jaguars, African leopards, Siberian tigers, European lynx, and Clouded leopards, all awaiting transfer to their permanent homes as they were completed. Llamas and Guanaco had been purchased from Whipsnade where the Curator, Victor Manton, had been one of the very first in the British zoo community to be helpful and take Marwell seriously. Disappointingly, some promised star animals like Red pandas and Red kangaroos had failed to arrive, thus adding to the reasons for visitor dissatisfaction because they were pictured in the beautiful and expensive first guide book. It was amazing how many visitors claimed to have come especially to see the missing animals!

Bird species at that time included a surprisingly comprehensive collection of the flightless birds known as ratites. We had Rheas, Emus, a lone Single-wattled cassowary and six young Ostrich. Cranes too were well represented, with East and West African crowned cranes as well as Lilford cranes. Three fabulous Kori bustards completed the roster of large birds. Deer of three species were also amongst the ruminants present at the outset.

Part of the initial plan was to group animals within areas approximating to the continents of their forebears. This 'zoogeographic' layout proved to be far too constraining for a zoo in its infancy and had to be abandoned early on. Several other factors added to the difficulties of 22nd May 1972 and the weeks that followed. One of these was that because of the considerable size of the Park – 2 miles around the perimeter road – I had decided that as well as pedestrians we would admit visitors in their cars, at an extra charge. What I had not anticipated was that by 1972 many people had become accustomed to the 'safari park' experience where all the limited numbers of species they exhibited were viewed from cars. The Marwell experience was meant to be different, with the cars only intended to ease tired feet. This was not appreciated by early visitors, some of whom took a quick drive round and departed convinced that there were no animals. I quickly found myself the subject of complaints both directly ('Get yourself some animals' was one memorable parting shot from a visitor) and in the press, which was the very last thing a struggling new zoo needed.

The situation was not helped by the attitude of such animals as we had succeeded in placing in their permanent accommodation. They wanted more time to adjust to new housing and they did not like the cold, wet weather of that early summer, and anyway they apparently had no wish to expose themselves to the public gaze! Neither they, nor many of the commendably idealistic staff, felt that my despairing demand that visitors should be allowed a peek at some animals was remotely reasonable. Every time I tried to enforce some reasonable acknowledgement of what a paying customer might legitimately expect, I was made to feel like a steely hearted money-grabber. To a lesser extent I have had to cope with this attitude throughout my zoo career, as I know have many of my peers. Money may not be the root of all evil but it certainly exerts powerful pressures! Western urban dwellers somehow expect viewing animals to be a little like a television programme and have little or no awareness of the impact on animals of weather. I have been told that during the wet seasons in African parks, when the animals can find water away from the pump-filled pools close to the visitor routes and consequently are not on view, complaints from tourists are long and loud!

I have sometimes thought how nice it would be to enjoy animals without the constraints imposed by the need to finance the pleasure of their company. However, that is not a practical proposition. For one thing it would presume a level of philanthropy not noticeably present in the human race and, for another, it would be like acquiring great paintings and squirrelling them away from public gaze. In the first edition of the rather cornily named *Marwell Zoos Paper*, which was sent to that early group of visitors who appreciated what I was seeking to achieve and who were to be the founders of the wonderful support group that became the Marwell Zoological Society, I was able to write: 'Two days short of a month since opening day, all the animals which we intended to exhibit in the first phase were in their permanent quarters except Lynx, Leopard, Jaguar and Cuban flamingos, together with the elusive Red pandas and Kangaroos.' In fact we were destined never to have the Red kangaroos. Grey kangaroos, however, came later – and the Red pandas came *much* later.

There is much received wisdom concerning the operation of zoos. One of these is that retail sales of appropriate goods, in the form of souvenirs of a visit, are a vital part of the necessary income stream for the maintenance of the operation. This knowledge hit us rather late in our planning so that the Portakabin, which was acquired and installed in a great rush, was at best a poor attempt at retailing and at worst a haven for small boys and not so small people of both sexes who lacked a proper appreciation of the normal ethical way of acquiring goods! Our first source of goods for resale was the Ravensden Zoo Company. At that time Ravensden were primarily wild animal dealers, from whom some of our early animals had been purchased, but who also used their contacts to operate a zoo souvenir business. In our haste we left it to them to send us a suitable supply of saleable goods. The revulsion which my wife Margaret and I felt as we opened case after case of ghastly plastic and tasteless rubber goods, some directly connected to animal themes and some less obviously so, remains with us still. A telephone call to Barry Papé, the proprietor of Ravensden, produced neither sympathy nor remorse. How could we, mere novices that we were, question his experience as to the tastes of the great British zoo-going public? Notwithstanding these reassurances, we sent back some items, such as crocodiles made of thin and therefore rather sharp plastic, as not being in any way the image that our brave new Park wished to project. Suffice to say that Mr Papé was right and we were hopelessly out of tune with the tastes of our visitors.

Once the word got around that there was a great opportunity at Marwell for purveyors of even faintly zoo-related merchandise, we were besieged by silver-tongued sales people, all expressing great admiration for our pioneering venture and wishing only to assist it by offering highly marketable goods at unbelievably advantageous prices! We soon began to dread the endless suitcases full of these great opportunities, and the time that every sales visit took. In this matter I was far less attentive than the importance of the shop warranted. Thankfully, Margaret was blessed with more patience and it is thanks to her interest and determination, not only with sales people, but also with shop staff, that we got started in retailing and that this was to grow in profit and scope from that first year onwards.

The opening date was planned to enable us to generate much-needed income from the 1972 spring bank holiday and the following week of local schools' half-term holidays. That holiday brought a flood of visitors and certainly provided a break in the financial cloud that was beginning to follow me everywhere. It also brought total chaos as no facility was large enough to cope with the numbers who came on the Monday. With an unusual insight into the reality of our 'building site apology for a zoo' (as it was perceived by numerous visitors) I had started the practice of issuing a note to each visitor expressing regret for our present state and promising the bearer a free return visit at a later date. This certainly saved us from what would have been a public relations disaster, to say nothing of potentially violent scenes. That these same innocent pieces of paper would come to haunt us at a later date, when it transpired that they were being exchanged for money in the local pubs, was not then as important as saving our good name.

The first place to suffer from the wave of visitors was the still unfinished and therefore inadequate car park. This was the front line, so like all leaders I threw myself into dealing with this problem and commenced a quarter of a century of car-parking duty on busy bank holidays, a task never anticipated with joy! I well knew that any car disappearing, because it could not be parked with its load of would-be visitors, was an important piece of revenue lost! A busy car park is a great place to learn something of the species that is neither confined nor endangered, but when it comes to parking cars is anxious to demonstrate that it is truly the most dangerous animal on Earth! There are only two kinds of car-parkers: the quick and the dead. Some drivers roar into their places at vast speed as though the whole zoo might blow away before they get in unless they are speedy, and they care not whoever might be mown down in the process, whilst others proceed with such caution that a huge queue of cars builds up behind them, destined in their turn to cause unmanageable chaos.

Whilst reflecting on the human race, a few other observations made in this first year, and confirmed over the subsequent years, are appropriate here. Marwell has (like all serious zoos) been open every day of the year except Christmas Day almost from its beginning, and yet the most frequent telephone enquiry from the public (even on fine summer bank holidays) is: 'Are you open?' I long cherished a wish to say: 'Only on wet Thursdays in November', but financial good sense always held me back! So-called joke phone calls are also a continuing feature of zoo life, reaching a peak on 1st April. There comes a time when enquiries for Messrs G. Raffe and C. Lion cease to amuse!

As I have already mentioned, the safari park concept of visitors driving round without appreciating the need to alight from their cars was a source of concern and a mystery as to how this could be remedied. Soon we learned that, in the cause of visitor satisfaction, every car driver should be told at the place of admission that to make the most of their visit they should park on the left-hand side of the road from time to time, get out and look at the animals. This did not deter one bright young man in a still brighter open-top sports car, accompanied by a rather fetching young lady, from enquiring as to whether or not it was safe to enter with an open-top vehicle. This was on a busy summer day when pedestrians were streaming in through an entrance gate parallel with that for vehicles. Perhaps he thought we had hit on a brilliant idea for maintaining carnivores at low cost, whilst at the same time providing a spectacle for our visitors reminiscent of Ancient Rome! One day shortly after the opening a school teacher was seen to be leading her little class up a slope towards the building site of the uncompleted restaurant. When challenged she said that she was obeying the signs which said 'Park on the left'!

While I will always look back on that summer of 1972 with a degree of horror, as I recall muddy clays of various hues, dissatisfied visitors and disappointing income, I also remember that many good and exciting things happened. The animals eventually entered into the spirit of what we were all about, and there were births of European lynx, and Plains, Grevy's and Hartmann's mountain zebras, which meant that early in our life we had notched up another unusual achievement by breeding, as well as keeping, three species of zebra. Keeping three species of zebra was a pretty unusual thing to do but I felt that demonstrating the very significant differences between the main species was educationally valuable, especially as all but the

Plains zebras, in their many forms, are endangered and were then all too often neglected in zoos. Although early visitors sometimes complained of there being too many zebras and deer (having failed to appreciate the significant difference between deer and antelope – another educational hurdle which I think we jumped early on) the policy has stood the test of time. Today Marwell is entrusted with the international studbooks for both Hartmann's and Grevy's zebras, and is actively involved in the conservation of the latter in their shrinking native habitat.

There were births among the antelope, with our flagship animal the Scimitar-horned oryx producing one male calf, and Impala, Nyala and Ellipsen waterbuck also making contributions as did our single female Blackbuck, who alas produced yet another male at a time when females were urgently needed. Arrivals after the opening included Demoiselle and Sarus cranes, a pair of Brazilian tapirs and more Bennett's wallabies from Whipsnade.

One of our more unusual acquisitions was in the very large shape of a male European wild boar who had been 'arrested' by police in the Basingstoke area where he had been found quietly munching his way through cabbages on local allotments. Ian Maddock and I collected him from a pig farm where he had been placed in custody and took him back to a hastily converted building where he was destined to spend the rest of his life. We never discovered his story, although a female of the same species was found shot only a mile away from the place of arrest. From this we concluded that, as so often happens with animals, they had once been somebody's idea of unusual pets that then outgrew their interest and keeping abilities. The boar was named Coulson in honour of our very helpful local policeman, though we never told either the animal or the constable! Most importantly for a struggling new zoo was the local and national newspaper coverage that Coulson gave us. Like any business seeking to attract the public, we needed people to hear about us and this was often hard and sometimes disappointing work. One particularly galling piece of PR going wrong just when we needed some really good publicity was a photograph of a Przewalski's horse, mare and foal in the *Daily Telegraph* which was attributed to Marwell Zoological Park but placed us *near Windsor*!

The beginning of an age of enlightenment in zoos' management of their animal collections was another feature of that summer of 1972. Before Marwell opened Dick van Dam, then Director of Rotterdam Zoo, contacted me to arrange a meeting to discuss a possible exchange of Przewalski's horses. At that time, still struggling with the day job, I frequently travelled to Holland and was duly met at Rotterdam Airport by Dick and his curator. It was another of my fortuitous meetings, for we immediately saw in each other kindred spirits and began a long personal and professional friendship. The immediate result of this was that a female Przewalski's named Taki (the Mongolian name for the species) came to Marwell from Rotterdam and a stallion, Vedran, went to Rotterdam. Dick travelled with Taki and liked what we were doing well enough to promise me a pair of Sumatran tigers to travel back to Marwell after we delivered Vedran to Blijdorp – as the Rotterdam Zoo is known. Money did not enter into our exchanges and that was unusual in those days. Dick van Dam, like me, had not spent his whole career in zoos and came to the profession with refreshing new philosophies which were to move not only his own institution into the second half of the 20th century, but also the whole respectable zoo community. As a leader amongst European zoos and as President of the International Union of Zoo Directors (now the World Association of Zoos & Aquariums or WAZA for short), Dick was destined to lead the movement to manage endangered species as one population regardless of their zoo of residence and ownership.

After the spring bank holiday week visitors became more than thin on the ground and those demon money worries returned with a vengeance. The painful process of 'letting people go' (to use a dreadful Americanism) began with the departure of a former freelance photographer who had joined as a marketing/PR person with enormous enthusiasm but a rather unrealistic view of what was needed to keep us afloat. The main summer holiday time had, however, brought us enough visitors to reassure myself and Margaret and, more importantly, the dear old NatWest bank and its long-suffering bank manager (and staunch friend), John Ellis, that we had a future. Treetops Restaurant was finished for the main summer holiday period, but not in time to help significantly with its own or the rest of the Park's finances. This led to yet another bad decision of mine of the kind that worrying situations produce. An expensive building standing in a potentially attractive site was going to earn no money to speak of until the next season, so Ken (our ex-publican catering manager) had the bright idea that, with a little further investment in a bar, cellar and the other accoutrements of a fancy eatery, we could make a small fortune. He was sure that a brewery would fund all of this, at a modest rate of interest and with a commitment by Marwell to buy all its beverages from their company at attractive (to the brewery) prices. Still better, he could procure chefs, chefs' sidekicks and waiters. Desperate times lead to desperate deeds and for a very short time Marwell became a high-class restaurant wanting for nothing but some clientele! Although we and a few friends enjoyed one or two good meals, the venture was short-lived as was the career at Marwell of the manager and his staff!

1972 finally wound down with a Christmas meal in the Hall, cooked by Margaret and my mother for keepers and curators on duty. This was consumed with a voraciousness indicative either of the poor rewards or of the healthy lifestyle enjoyed by our staff! Exceptionally for this and some other early Christmas Days, we chose to depart from the conventional closing because we so desperately needed every penny. To spare our gatekeepers, we placed an honesty box and suitable sign at the entrance. To our surprise there were a few score of visitors, no doubt many, like me, having no great love of the festive season. Although this device gathered a little extra revenue, we stopped after only a few years for two reasons. Firstly, we found that, even in the season of goodwill, some people did not enter into the spirit with honesty and the amount of money in the box nowhere near tallied with the number of bodies seen wandering around the Park. Much more seriously, all Park rules were broken in the absence of normal entrance supervision, with free-roaming dogs coming close to creating serious accidents to animals which were not used to being barked at.

My first year as a zoo owner also taught me much about the public and *their* animals. Initially we banned dogs from the Park which is a rule that remains in force to this day. However, the sight of a lady parading past our leopards with an African grey parrot on her shoulder, then another carrying a cat in a basket and yet another with a tame monkey, caused a rethink of the signs at the entrance for, as these folk pointed out, we had only advertised a ban on *dogs*. Signs were quickly changed to *'No Pets'*.

In the main it was – and still is – dogs that cause the most worry to zoo managers. There are those owners who are so obsessed with their pets that they will not visit the zoo if 'dear Toby' cannot share the experience, and those who find fault with the kennels provided for dogs who are not too precious to be left outside. Worse still are those owners who leave their pets in a closed car on a hot day. Most astonishing of all are the folk who bowl into the car park on a busy day and demand to be parked in the shade, happily oblivious of the fact that the sun changes position in the course of a day!

With so many lessons learnt in those first few months, so many worries and so many difficulties overcome, and such a relief still to be in existence – that was Marwell at the end of 1972. An influx of visitors on New Year's Day 1973 (for which again we were ill-prepared) gave us renewed faith and vigour for the first full year which had just begun.

Chapter 7

By the spring of 1973 Marwell was beginning to look like a real zoo. Money had been found to surface most of the roads with tarmacadam, thus reducing the clinging mud which had been such a negative aspect of the earlier visitor experience. Building work continued, as indeed it has for the life of Marwell, but it was at last possible to contain it to defined areas so that it was not visually dominating everywhere. Most importantly for myself and the growing zoo, a small Norwich-based merchant bank took a look at the company of which I had been a 50 per cent founder, Anglian Food Group, and decided that if its success had been achieved by two simple farmers from Essex and Norfolk then really clever people with Harvard Business School backgrounds could do really great things. Very happily I sold my remaining shares to feed the ever-present capital needs of Marwell, and as the clever people clearly had no use for an eccentric whose devotion to another cause was very obvious, I was freed from the day job.

Interestingly, the 'clever' people fairly quickly managed to bankrupt the old firm, confirming the view that I had developed whilst working in America of Harvard-based business management doctrines. Further confirmation of these views was to come later in my zoo years, as management types sought to find complex solutions to simple problems. I will always remain a disciple of the old farming saying: 'There is no dung like the master's foot' – a management style that has served me well throughout my life.

Births have always given me a buzz and by our second year they were becoming regular occurrences. A small group of African hunting dogs were our first non-feline carnivores. Then, as now, this much misunderstood species was considered endangered. In the strict zoological sense they are not dogs at all but are a species more closely allied to Hyenas than to those companions of mankind known by the rather charming scientific name of *Canis familiaris*. Our first litter of these was born by Caesarean section which, of course, necessitated anaesthetising the mother who, after recovery, showed no interest in her offspring. Of the nine puppies extracted from their mother's womb, six responded to life-giving support. We then lost one more in a vain effort to stimulate the mother's interest and milk. We then tried feeding the survivors with artificial milk designed for dog puppies, but it soon became obvious that this was not suitable for the special needs of these youngsters so we hit on the idea of seeking a domestic bitch that had just given birth to unwanted puppies. Our friends in local television, the BBC and the commercial channel Southern Television, broadcast an appeal on our behalf, and we soon had in our care a very gentle mongrel bitch with the very inappropriate name of Sly, together with one of her own pups. Sly took to her extra task with great enthusiasm and saw her extra family through to a healthy six weeks by which time the wild puppies' teeth, so necessary for a hunter's life in the wild, were too sharp for her comfort.

A cold wet first day of May brought us another orphan who was destined to grab a large place in the hearts of all who knew him, and bring Marwell a great deal of much-needed good publicity. Nimana, one of three young Siberian tigers that had come to us from Leipzig, had done what wild feline mothers often do at a first birth – she had panicked and spread three full-term cubs around the damp and chilly paddock. The keeper in charge of that section quickly saw what had happened during his early morning inspection and immediately secured the bewildered mother in an inside den and then searched the outside enclosure where he found two sad little corpses and one sodden bundle which was showing faint signs of life. This he brought into Marwell Hall where the little furry ball quickly aroused Margaret's maternal instincts and her practical skills as a trained nurse. After a good rubbing which served both to clean and stimulate the little male, he was placed in the warming oven of the Aga in the Hall's vast kitchen where he soon began to recover and became strong enough to take some nourishment from a hypodermic syringe. Tigger – as the little animal was named by devotees of the Christopher Robin books (almost immediately shortened to Tig) – soon took to an artificial milk diet suckled through human baby bottles, a vast number of which were donated by a local nursing home. Marwell was by then already attracting a fund of local goodwill which helped its growth so much and which was in such contrast to the opposition encountered at the beginning.

Apart from initial hair loss which is a common occurrence with artificially reared wild cats, Tig's health gave us little cause for concern. He took his food readily from a number of us, although Margaret remained his favourite person throughout his long life. He hated being left on his own and we had the idea of providing him with a playmate by borrowing a lion cub from Windsor Safari Park (now Legoland) then owned by the Billy Smart circus family, who were hand rearing a great number of lion cubs. Probably because he was used to being one of many, Dougal – as we named him – was no gentleman and had developed competitive skills early in his young life which Tig had not. Our lad stood back while Dougal pushed him around at meal and play times which very soon resulted in him losing weight, so Dougal was speedily returned whence he came and Tig was given more freedom in the Hall where he had access to both the offices and our living quarters. Most people enjoyed having a tiger around, although my mother found his habit of biting her ankles troublesome and was even less pleased when, at the end of a visit by my parents, Tig unpacked their luggage while they were at breakfast!

My parents, who had watched my career to date with a mixture of pride and trepidation, had accepted the zoo as being just one more stage in my unpredictable progress through life. Mother enjoyed her visits (apart from Tig) but by our first year Father, a man who once had a keen scientific mind, had largely lost his grasp on reality. One day at the height of my money worries I took him to see some of the animals on a day that was singularly bereft of visitors. He turned to me and said that if I opened the Park to visitors I could probably make some money. It was a sadness to me that he died a year later without knowing what his wayward offspring had accomplished.

One member of the household who determinedly and successfully ignored Tig's presence was our aged black labrador, Silky, an animal who devoted her life solely and wholeheartedly to food, despite having an arthritic hip which would have benefited from a strict diet. Controlling Silky's food intake was impossible with an animal that easily found so many opportunities to acquire food, either by stealing what was intended for other animals or, as happened in good weather when families brought picnics into the Park, by sitting beside them with that appealing look so well known to all who have shared a part of their lives with a labrador. Hers was a charmed life, for although she had only encountered sheep and cattle in her early years, she frequently crossed paddocks with ostriches, antelope and zebras without misadventure.

Tig's first public appearance was with that remarkable wildlife artist David Shepherd at an event in Marwell Hall to launch *Tiger Fire*, the first of the limited edition prints that David donated to raise money for the World Wildlife Fund. The contrast between the cuddly tiger cub photographed in his arms and the fierce animal portrayed in the painting was enormous, but both helped spread the message that all races of tiger then, as now, were struggling to maintain a presence in their natural habitats. This was followed by an adoption by the crew of the Portsmouth-based cruiser HMS *Tiger*, resulting in a great photo opportunity (a phrase with which we were to grow all too familiar), with the little cub surrounded by sailors. Tig was not able to accompany us when Margaret and I had a very enjoyable dinner in the wardroom of that ship. This was not long after HMS *Tiger* had hosted a meeting between Prime Minister Harold Wilson and Ian Smith, then Premier of Rhodesia, as they attempted to solve the problems of UDI. Little was said of that occasion other than for our hosts to point out that they had chosen not to follow the usual convention of hanging Wilson's portrait in their wardroom!

One publicity stunt to which we subjected Tig took us, and him, away from the zoo. It was in retrospect very amusing but was not at the time a happy experience. We were invited to take part in a midday television show with Terry Wogan, who was then at the beginning of his fame. This was to be live at a commercial television studio in Birmingham. So with the three-month-old Tig in a comfortable crate on the back seat of my Rolls-Royce (which was yet to be sold to fund more Grevy's zebras) Margaret and I set out early one fine summer morning, armed with food and drink for the three of us, feeling that this was a wonderful PR opportunity for our crucial second summer season.

More than anything the experience was, for us, a study of human reaction to unusual circumstances. Our first stop was at a service station on the M4 to give Tig a chance to have a drink of milk and relieve himself. We walked him briefly around a car park crowded with early morning travellers who, without exception, looked away as if embarrassed or fearful that some ghastly trick was being played on them. In the centre of Birmingham we stopped the car to ask directions to the studio from a thickset man wearing a butcher's apron who obliged with a flow of words delivered in that strange nasal tone that the citizens of that fine city use. While this good man was in full flood, Tig, who had remained totally silent so far on the journey, started an earth-shattering complaint, made all the louder by the resonance of his travelling box, nearly drowning out the good man's directions. Never once by so much as a facial twitch did our informant indicate the remotest curiosity as to whom or what we might be carrying in our upmarket vehicle.

The next human contact was with the heavily made-up manageress of the studio's canteen. Studio reception staff were rather chilly, but we were assured that all three of us would receive a warm welcome at this busy place and be given whatever refreshment we desired. With total confidence, therefore, that two people with a tiger would be particularly welcome, I approached this important personage in the canteen and requested a bowl of slightly warmed milk, only to be met with a frozen stare and another nasal flow of words to the effect that no animals were ever to cross her precious threshold. Even the fact that our companion was to star with Terry made no impression on this harridan. Eventually we found a person in higher authority who lodged us in a dressing room and organised some room service. By this time all three of us were feeling rather uptight. Tension however soon gave way to naughty pleasure as Tig set about destroying the wallpaper and shower curtains.

When our moment of fame came Tig and I were seated by ourselves for a moment before Terry rushed in wearing a Victorian lion tamer's uniform and cracking a whip. With that bit of theatricality over we had a short chat about Tig in particular and the status of tigers generally.

Tig, as I have so often observed with animals of all kinds, behaved immaculately while the cameras were on us. However, he did have the last word, in a manner of speaking, as I was putting him back into his travelling box for the journey home. He bit me intentionally but quite gently on my hand, which was the only time in our long association when he meant it! An Elastoplast was all the first aid needed for a wound that I rather treasured as a token of our ability to communicate with each other.

Tig made many more television appearances, but from then on always at Marwell, in surroundings with which he was familiar. One of these was an hilarious film sequence with the children's television series *Magpie* where, on a day of pouring rain, bowls of milk which were being offered to a by this time sizeable tiger, slid off a large table built for tigers to rest on, repeatedly soaking the stars. This had a number of repeat showings and was the beginning of a long association that Marwell and I had with that programme until it was discontinued. Tig also helped with an income tax problem. Because I then had income from sources unconnected with Marwell that was being channelled into the zoo I received a visit from an Inspector of Taxes who queried my contention that breeding wild animals was a business. Placing a tiger cub in his arms was at least as persuasive as my passionate arguments!

Media exposure is something that all zoos seek, both to attract paying visitors to come and see more, and to establish the kind of 'street cred' that may lead to sponsorships and (hopefully) legacies. As I write this in the last years of the first decade of the 21st century there are at least four television series based on British zoos, and worldwide there are now many such regular broadcasts to feed the multitude of hungry channels. I believe most of these benefit all zoos and, more importantly, stimulate interest in the whole animal kingdom. Cynics, however, enjoy pointing out that animals are more cooperative and less expensive than actors.

A quarter of a century ago when we filmed a series at Marwell on endangered species for *Magpie*, the work was much harder than it would be today, partly because of less advanced film and sound technology and also because those were the days of large, unionised crews. I cannot remember a sequence with *Magpie*'s Jenny Handley,

Above: My meeting with Khrushchev. Myself and a chicken in the grip of power.

Below: Walter Stone – the man who opened a big door in my life.

Above: Roland Lindemann (right) – a wise teacher.

Below: Marwell Hall – a stately white elephant.

Right: Margaret with Tig at eighteen months.

Below: Tig with the author. Our first very precious birth.

Above: Leopards need trees.

Below: Kurten, father of Tig and many more cubs.

Above: Marwell's Wonderful Railway passes Greater kudu and White rhino.

Below: Scimitar horned oryx – Marwell's proud symbol species.

Left: Roo – our next baby.

Below: A Grevy zebra – better than a Rolls Royce!

Above: Prezwalski's horses at Marwell.

Below: My sixtieth birthday marquee.

Above & below: A few days later a little more comfort in a yurt.

Above: Domestic camels in Mongolia Gobi B.

Below: Vladimir Spitsin and assistant in the old Moscow zoo.

Above: Saharan convoy in Niger.

Below: My last view of Basil in the San Diego Wild Animal Park.

Above: A Snow leopard. The most charismatic of all the big cats.

Below: Roan antelope at Marwell. Parents of those to return to Swaziland.

Above: The author and Hamish Currie in Swaziland.

Below: Ted Reilly; Swaziland's conservationist supreme and my hero, with a pet Hyrax

Above: Leaders of modern zoo/conservation thought: Bill Conway, Director Emeritus of the World Conservation Society (left) and Nate Flesness, creator of the International Species Information System (ISIS).

Below: Tom Foose and Ulie Seal (centre) in Moscow zoo at the time of the fruitless first attempt at a reintroduction programme.

Above: The wild always called me. Grevy zebras at the Lewa Conservancy, where a quarter of the non-zoo population can be found.

Below: Heroes of the Marwell Zimbabwe Trust. Director Verity Bowman and Trustee and wildlife vet par excellence Dr Chris Foggin.

Above: Creating an Okapi house. The problem piles of soil.

Below: An Okapi. To me a magical beast.

Above: The Princess Royal inspects the penguins after opening Penguin World.

Below: Some of Marwell's paddocks. Rhino and Kudu in the foreground and Scimitar horned oryx in the distance.

who was a wonderful presenter to work with, without some minor squabble because some unauthorised person had moved a sign or a light, or a shot had been spoilt by an unscripted epithet from an unnecessary crew member. Despite these problems some good film was shot. Jenny and I even did a Christmas spoof film wherein we solemnly discussed the endangered status of pantomime horses in a field with three of these creatures, one of whom showed considerable aggression towards us.

The year after having Tig as a baby in our house, Margaret and I were presented with a tiny, shrivelled and seriously ugly orphan and into our lives came (A.A. Milne again) Roo. She was a very young Bennett's wallaby whose mother had died. I said in my all-knowing way: 'Let us do our best with this one, but don't worry about getting fond of it because wallabies are not very bright.' How wrong can one be? After an initial struggle to get her to take milk substitute whilst living in a ladies' shoulder bag, warmed by a hot-water bottle, she developed into a most charming companion. She was slow to take solid foods. We tried everything that we could think of to tempt her, but nothing appealed until one evening we had some friends in for drinks, accompanied by nibbles which included prawn cocktail-flavoured crisps. Some of these spilled and Roo ate them with gusto, and for at least another month these were her main solid sustenance. When she appeared on *Magpie* the studio provided her with a plastic bag containing enough bags of these crisps to see her into adulthood. Predictably she moved onto more suitable food shortly afterwards!

Local radio also claimed its share of Marwell input. I recall a few occasions when BBC's Radio Solent asked me to be part of a small panel answering phoned-in questions. One of these floored me totally when a listener sought our views on the absence in schools of Nit Nurses. I had no idea that such creatures had ever existed! Fortunately other panel members were not so ignorant and I learnt that whilst they were less abundant than formerly, they were not endangered! Another such panel was at the time of the US Senate's Watergate investigation. When asked if Nixon should resign I was very emphatic that he should. I was then severely admonished by a bishop who accused me of prejudging the poor man. We had quite a little contretemps which would have made for a good broadcast except, unfortunately, this was being pre-recorded and at the end of our half-hour we were told that the equipment had failed to capture any of our words and would we please do it all again. We did, but of course all the fire had gone out of us by then. Incidentally, Nixon resigned some five days later rather than face impeachment.

In later years Tig's mother Nimana and her sister Amaga went on to produce and rear many litters. Together with the cub's father, Leipzig-born Kurten, we were able to have a delightful exhibit of the two sisters and their offspring, together with father, all happily sharing the same enclosure. Whilst tigers in the wild are usually solitary except for mothers and cubs, I believe this to be largely due to there being a much lower density of prey animals in most tiger habitats, than there is for lions in Africa. At Marwell where there was always ample food there was no reason for animals that knew each other well not to play Happy Families. We did, of course, have to manage a degree of separation at meal times!

The 'Leipzig Three' founded a dynasty, with offspring going to other zoos all around the world. Marwell and other zoos have become so successful at breeding Siberian tigers that breeding today is restricted to avoid overfilling the limited number of suitable zoo places, while at the same time planned so as to ensure the integrity of the species by careful genetic and demographic management. It is an irony that although captive breeding can ensure that tigers, and many other species, may never become extinct, their place in natural habitats is, at best, insecure. Of the tiger subspecies which existed on Earth at the beginning of the 20th century, two (the Javan and the Persian) have been lost for ever but might have been saved if some had been brought to zoos in time. Good management of endangered species in zoos can ensure that their unique genes are never irretrievably lost. In contrast, habitats are always vulnerable to human economic and political forces.

Boris and Lena, who had played such a pivotal part in starting my zoo career, never bred. Boris came with a kidney infection which shortened his life. Lena, curiously, developed ever larger white spots as she grew older. White tigers are commonly seen in zoos and safari parks and sometimes, misleadingly, they are referred to as endangered. In fact all the ones presently in zoos are the result of cross-breeding of two races of tigers in an American circus and are of no conservation importance. Lena, however, was pure Siberian and when her breeder, Robert Baudy, visited Marwell and saw her white spots he wanted to buy her back. I have always had sentimental feelings towards animals with which I have had a close association, and Lena was certainly not to go back to Florida.

For Tig we obtained a young mother-reared female from Rotterdam Zoo named Lara as a mate. Although they were compatible they were never (to use modern terminology) 'close' and consequently never bred. Towards the end of his days Tig was placed with his mother Nimana who was then, in our professional view, definitely retired from breeding duties. To our total surprise she produced (non-viable) cubs. Bill Hall, who was the second refugee from London Zoo when he joined our ranks as a Head Keeper, soon assumed the role of resident sage and wit and quickly named Tig 'Oedipus'!

Our first refugee from London Zoo was Peter Bircher who had written to me early in 1973 when he heard on the ever-busy zoo grapevine that the joint Curators, who had done such sterling work during the anxious days of waiting for planning permission, the build-up time and the troubling opening period, had resigned. Both were young men of great integrity and commitment to conservation and animal welfare. Both found the commercial pressures of needing to attract visitors and their money impossible to reconcile with their beliefs. Consequently I had a particularly stressful time when I was both Curator and Director, and a part of that period encompassed the last of my business days. Peter had been an inspector with the RSPCA before becoming a veterinary assistant in the animal hospital at London Zoo. His application was strengthened by an endorsement from David Jones, then veterinary surgeon at London Zoo's country animal park at Whipsnade. David and I were destined to have a long association involving Marwell and the two London zoos, but that was still way in the future. At interview Peter came over as competent and enthusiastic and as he was, truth be told, the only applicant, he joined us in the summer of 1973. Peter and I did not always see eye to eye but we worked well together and he continued as General Curator up to and after my retirement in 1998. Marwell, which has never stopped growing, owes him a great deal.

The animal collection grew throughout those early days, both through births and by acquisition. I had always planned to have all the antelope species at Marwell that belonged to the family Hippotraginae (meaning 'horse-like') to which our already established Scimitar-horned oryx belonged. From that family Frans van den Brink offered me a group of Gemsbok which had to be collected from the port of Walvis Bay in Namibia and brought on the *Worcester Castle* to Liverpool and thence to quarantine in Manchester. Thinking that it would be a good experience for a young man who had just left school, I sent my younger son Simon to accompany them, having instructed him how to inspect the animals before accepting them. Unfortunately, when he arrived in Windhoek he found the animals already crated and was given no opportunity to view them. As it turned out, these animals had literally been caught from the wild, crated and dispatched. Tragically, all of the females were pregnant and all aborted on the ship. Instead of a beneficial experience Simon had a voyage from hell and understandably lost interest in the zoo world. Such an experience was part of a darker age of zoo-keeping which should never be repeated in our more enlightened times. Happily, from those animals a breeding group came to Marwell after quarantine and the species has flourished in the zoo ever since.

My absorption into the British zoo community happened surprisingly quickly, thanks in part to Geoffrey Schomberg's advocacy of Marwell's potential and my known American connections. I believe that it was also seen in my favour that I had taken time during the year prior to opening to visit several of the major German zoos on both sides of the Wall which then so cruelly divided Germany, and made the acquaintance of some of their famous directors. I had also taken two precious days just before our opening to attend the first conference on breeding endangered species in captivity hosted by Gerald Durrell's Jersey Zoo. There I met more professional colleagues and there I was made aware of a second British zoo group. Its membership was comprised largely, but not wholly, of the commercial zoos and safari parks and was opposed to the Zoo Federation's goal of introducing legislation to raise the standards of all British zoos. Such legislation was badly needed as, truth to tell, there were then many very poor zoos in Britain. Unfortunately the legacy of these remains in the minds of an older generation who visited such zoos decades ago, and to this day seem unaware of changed times.

It was to be many years before the Zoo Licensing Act was passed into law. This was as a result of much work by the Federation, in which I am proud to have played a very full part. Prior to this Act, the Federation, like many professional and trade bodies, had its own system of inspections to qualify a zoo for membership. The inspectors were directors, curators and veterinary surgeons from member institutions. Marwell was inspected and passed within weeks of opening and I soon found myself involved with the affairs of the Federation and becoming an inspector myself. After a little more than a year of directing a zoo open to the public, I was asked to be one of the inspectors for Edinburgh Zoo, which had a much larger and more diverse animal collection than my own. This had first opened in 1913 and it seemed to me that, some 60 years later, it had remained frozen in that time period. All the buildings were typical of a Victorian menagerie with a centrepiece mansion distinctly of that era which, however, contained a magnificent restaurant for members of the society which owned the zoo. There we inspectors were very well lunched.

Two memories of that visit which, happily, was destined to be the first of many, are forever fresh in my mind. One was that the male keeping staff wore caps with shiny peaks and gaiters! The other is of a large house with a number of Chimpanzees, all housed singly or as one-sex couples in separate iron-barred cages. All this was soon to change. One reason for the inspection was the appointment of Roger Wheater as the new Director, with a mandate from his council to bring the zoo into the second half of the 20th century. Roger had taken up the directorship after leaving the post of Director of National Parks in Uganda when that country was in the grip of Idi Amin's madness. Roger succeeded brilliantly in his new task, and soon played a major role in the reshaping of the British and international zoo world. Happily, we were destined to be friends and colleagues, working together for beneficial change in many arenas.

My involvement in what might be regarded as extramural activities met my personal need for a challenge beyond what could be achieved within the limitations of my own patch. All my life I have sought a large stage, and the changes that I felt the zoo world needed gave me reasons and opportunities enough. Time spent outside the perimeter fence also brought many benefits to Marwell, both directly and indirectly. In present-day business jargon this would be described as 'opportunities to think and learn outside the box'.

The second International Conference on the Breeding of Endangered Species in Captivity was held at London Zoo in July 1976, at which I was invited to give a paper on 'The Economics of Breeding Endangered Species'. As the Zoological Society of London was founded 150 years before the year of the conference, I should have felt daunted to be speaking with the experience of a mere seven-year newcomer! However I did not feel like that and happily (and cockily) embraced a task which brought, as an unexpected bonus, an opportunity to have a species at Marwell which had long been on my wanted list but always seemed way out of reach. Lady Luck once more smiled on me, for although I have no pretence to either oratorical or wordsmith talents, I managed a paper for this occasion which was remarkably well received and earned the approval and the friendship of Illka Koivisto, then the director of Helsinki Zoo, which was one of the very few institutions then having success with the species of feline that is the most beautiful in grace, temperament and (to its cost) appearance: the Snow leopard. Illka offered Marwell a female and promised that as his zoo was also the international studbook keeper for the species, he would help me to find a mate for her.

Despite having many reservations about circuses I visited many in my pre-Marwell days, simply because of my interest in animals. Thus it happened that at some time in the late 1950s or early 1960s I visited the Sir Robert Fosset's circus where Bailey Fosset presented a remarkable mixed group of big cats, which included Jaguars, Black and Spotted leopards, Pumas and two really beautiful Snow leopards. The only part that these two animals played in the show was to sit demurely on their pedestals whilst other animals performed and then, as the last to leave, they exited with their trainer holding their fabulous tails as handles. The whole performance was carried out in a quiet and friendly manner, which gave no hint of the harshness so often associated with this kind of act, although the mixing of species so foreign to each other in nature must have taken more than patience alone.

What I most recall was the excellent condition of these two animals in contrast to the two that I had seen in London Zoo, huddled together on a shelf in a small, bare cage at one end of the now long since demolished lion house. At the time of my circus visit the animals I saw were almost certainly caught in the wild which, with any other big cat, would make it remarkable that they submitted to a hands-on relationship with their trainer. Illka gave a valuable paper at the same conference about Helsinki's breeding successes and commented on how friendly their first individual (which was also taken from the wild) became after a time. I can personally attest to the fact that Snow leopards readily become friendly towards their keepers, a characteristic also found with Siberian tigers and Okapi. I have a theory that this is because these animals evolved in parts of the world sparsely occupied by human beings. To know us is to fear us.

A few months later I travelled to Helsinki to accompany Vilkku on her flight to London in a noisy, draughty cargo plane. She was not a young animal, so in my pride which was mixed with anxiety, I probably over-reacted by insisting that I travelled with her and carried with me an oxygen supply in case of any emergency. In reality she travelled more comfortably than I did. From such an unplanned but happy circumstance, this important species came to Marwell, where they have bred very well, as they have now done in many zoos to the point where breeding, as with tigers, has to be limited.

With some prescience I ended my paper for that conference with: 'There is in my view no way in which the breeding of endangered species can be made financially self-supporting.' I have seldom spoken or written truer words!

Chapter 8

Sometimes in life a very normal, maybe even humdrum, start to a day will so quickly be changed and develop such momentum that it will be a day remembered for the rest of a person's life. Such a day was Thursday, 15th September 1977. We were still living in the vastness of Marwell Hall at that time and, as was my practice, I had made an early inspection of the Park and most of its animals, as well as having the usual chats with staff members about the work in hand prior to taking a quick breakfast. Suddenly my park communication radio crackled with the news of a serious problem in the giraffe house. At that time this was a simple building, having only the year before been given a modest extension so that it would be possible to separate animals from each other in the event of injury, sickness or calving.

Awkwardly trapped in an internal corner, and very obviously experiencing discomfort from one leg which prevented any hope of rising by his own efforts, lay our breeding male Giraffe. Victor had come to us from where he had been born and was named after Victor Manton, curator of Whipsnade at the time. Giraffe are superbly adapted for a life of feeding at a level where there is no competition for the food source – namely leaves on the higher trees. However, as with all adaptations a positive comes with a negative (such as the price we humans pay for the advantages we derive from walking on our hind legs, which is our susceptibility to back problems). With Giraffe the penalty for their lofty larder access is difficulty in controlling their legs and neck whenever fate in one form or another places them in an unusual position. This is the only real problem with zoo care of these normally placid and manageable animals. Normally a minor wound or a medical condition which calls for hands-on attention in a mammal species is dealt with quickly and safely, for both animals and people, by the application of an immobilising drug. This is followed by the administration of an antagonist to the first drug which speedily has the patient back on his or her feet, with assistance for a short time by keepers until the animal is steady. Human intervention in the re-establishment of a Giraffe on its four feet, however, is extremely difficult without grave risk to animal and humans alike.

Victor's situation on that September morning was not immediately recognised as being especially grave. We did not know how he had come to be lying in such a difficult position and we felt sure that if we could pull and push him out of the awkward corner in which he was placed he would eventually be able to stand up. One encouraging aspect of the situation was that Victor himself remained totally calm, and indeed his attitude appeared to be slightly apologetic for causing so much trouble and being so unable to assist in our efforts to help him! However, where he was situated made it impossible for us to move the poor fellow, even though shortly after his plight had been discovered every able-bodied staff member had been mobilised. Neither did the layout of the building make it possible to employ any available mechanical aids. We paused in our efforts to consider what might be done while Victor happily chewed at leaves and bananas proffered by his many human friends. Someone suggested that we ask the Fire Brigade if they would try to help, by using the inflatable bags that are normally used to force metal apart in order to free people trapped in road accidents. So a call was made to the emergency service for a rather unusual form of help.

This call initiated a turn of events which was to have both short- and long-term effects beyond our imagination. Our only thoughts on that September day were directed at the re-establishment on four legs of one rather crestfallen male Giraffe. None of us at that time knew that the emergency channel calls are monitored by members of the press, so we were quite unprepared for the arrival on the scene of a full-blown television crew from Southern Television. It was headed by a rather aggressive producer who swept away my pleas for peace and quiet for the sake of the animal, by threatening to film the closed doors of the building and to ask the viewers to imagine just what might be going on behind them! Faced with this singularly unpleasant threat, we decided to let the film crew do their work, providing they did not obstruct the truly marvellous Fire Brigade staff, who had arrived shortly afterwards, or ourselves and our veterinary surgeon who, by this time, had administered mild sedatives and antibiotics to the still helpless but co-operative Victor. To be fair to the television people, they behaved impeccably after our initial spat. (I should record at this point that right from our earliest days at Marwell we enjoyed a friendly and generally supportive relationship with all branches of the local media, who always seemed to understand our commitment to conservation and the welfare of our charges.)

Our first move, with the help of the firemen and their airbags, was to manoeuvre Victor out of the house and onto the packed gravel of the outside yard where he would stand the best chance of obtaining a foothold and regaining both his standing position and his dignity. Once we had assured ourselves that a foothold was possible, *if* our poor friend could regain his strength, we set about the difficult task of ensuring that he was so positioned that he could rise if he were able and yet could not slip back again into a more seriously difficult position. We protected him against the chill autumnal night with straw bales and provided him with food and water which he took readily from his keepers. This in itself was surprising for, although born in a zoo and living his whole life in fairly close proximity to people, Victor, like all (except hand-reared) zoo animals, was not accustomed to very close proximity to people – because the last thing we want to do with our wild charges is turn them into something like domestic pets. At this time of crisis Victor seemed to understand that we were doing our best to help him. He even submitted readily to the antibiotic and pain-killing injections. Also some medication was administered in the time-honoured easy way with Giraffe (and some other species), which is by hiding the medicine in a banana. Addiction to bananas is another of those strange aspects of animal adaptation to the different opportunities that exist in a zoo to those of natural habitat. Bananas are very seldom available in Giraffe habitat.

Whilst the Marwell team was absorbed in our mission of care, we had failed to notice the growing band of television and other media folk who were gathering outside the giraffe enclosure. This was only, as we were to learn to our consternation, the first trickle of what was to become a global torrent of press interest in the struggle for Victor's health and life. This global interest had, as all things do, both positive and negative aspects. Positive was the potentially useful help that came our way. A local firm voluntarily offered scaffolding and lifting gear to help to raise the stricken animal. The Royal Navy sail makers at Portsmouth built a canvas cradle which would support Victor's weight as the machinery began a gentle lift. Less helpful were the offers that suggested everything from the laying-on of hands to the use of a helicopter. That particular suggestion came from many well-wishers, all of whom must have assumed that helicopters could be equipped with silencers. Animals are alarmed by unfamiliar noise, especially if they cannot see or understand where it is coming from. In this context it is interesting to note, however, that in later years when Marwell was honoured by visits from the Princess Royal, her helicopter landed, for security reasons, in the Giraffes' outdoor grass paddock and the Giraffe were amongst the most interested watchers of the royal visitor and totally unfazed by the arrival of her transport.

By Day Three of the struggle, the zoo's switchboard was totally jammed with a combination of advice-givers, well-wishers and the morbidly prurient wishing to be informed of sensational details. So overwhelming was the interest that, with our agreement, the zoo's telephone was disconnected which in turn caused a near shut-down of the Winchester exchange. Frustrated telephone folk then started to besiege London Zoo's phones. With only one exception, the world's zoos were supportive and told all enquirers that Marwell was doing all the right things for poor Victor. The exception was an American zoo director who offered obvious advice via the media and ultimately and very publicly offered a replacement Giraffe to us, whilst privately telling me how many thousands of dollars this would cost. I guess there is at least one such person in every profession!

This interest from across the Atlantic and from the rest of the world stemmed from the fact that, by the third day, Victor was a major news story and his ups and downs were being reported, I was later told, on every television channel in the world as well as on radio and in newsprint. First thing every morning for the duration of Victor's travail I met our local BBC television anchor, Bruce Parker, so that he could give an early news report for all the BBC's channels and affiliates.

The intensity of the media interest was truly amazing because, as I have already indicated, Giraffe are vulnerable and Victor was by no means the first or the last animal of his species, both in zoos and in the wild, to pay a heavy price for his evolutionary speciality. The explanation has to be the early arrival in the story of a television crew and a slow news time. The press were largely fair, and indeed often kind, although one or two cartoons relating his plight to such topical items as the difficulties of the new Concorde supersonic airliner and the Tory party were more than a little bizarre, especially to Victor's helpers for whom the outside world had largely ceased to exist. Throughout the long six days of his involuntary grounding, Victor remained calm and responsive to his favourite keeper Ruth Giles and veterinary surgeon John Walmsley. He seemed to realise that even the inevitably noisy erection of the lifting tower and the difficult insertion of the cradle beneath his large but stricken form were intended for his welfare.

The morning of Day Six found us with everything in place for our first attempt to raise Victor. The plan was that if we could once take his weight off the ground, possibly massage his legs and then slowly lower him, then perhaps very, very slowly those legs might once again learn to support and eventually carry his massive frame. We all felt that it was a near hopeless case, but Victor's seemingly relaxed attitude and the continued operation of his bodily functions spelt hope, or at the very least demanded that we gave him the best possible chance of a return to a full life. Had he not been so calm we would right at the beginning have given him a merciful end, although I have no doubt this would have brought us much unfavourable publicity.

The lifting process was begun slowly and carefully at around eleven in the morning of 20th September, with keepers Bill Hall and Ruth Giles, veterinary surgeon John Walmsley, curator Peter Bircher, assistant director David Aston and myself attending to his body systems and his rather unwieldy head and neck. Initially all went well, and for a few minutes we felt, almost for the first time, real hope. Sadly, that hope was not sustained and we were aware of that subtle change, known all too well by experienced animal people, that tells us that life has ebbed away.

Once death was certain, I was summoned to talk to the assembled press, some of whom had gone to extraordinary lengths to ensure good coverage. Photographers had brought in stepladders, whilst television cameras were elevated by hydraulically operated towers known as cherry pickers. There were more people surrounding the giraffe house than on a bank holiday Monday! Not usually either shy or intimidated, I confess that it was with more than a little difficulty that I remained dry-eyed as I addressed the whole press group and subsequently did a series of individual interviews for radio and television. Bill Hall and Ruth Giles were able to disappear quietly into the food store where no stiff upper lip was required. The next morning's newspapers gave Victor's decease front-page coverage. Writing in the *Daily Express* of 21st September Jean Rook gave a moving epitaph which began: 'He towered 18ft above our troubles. He rose above Northern Ireland, Rhodesia, a bread strike, and the deaths of Marc Bolan and Maria Callas.' She continued in a similar vein.

A post-mortem revealed that the cause of death was heart failure caused, no doubt, by the prolonged stress of unaccustomed proximity to human beings and unusual activities around his helpless form. The cause of his downfall was a torn adductor muscle (the one that all mammals have which pull legs inwards). The media chose to speculate that he fell in pursuit of a female and, of course, that made a good press story, but we had no evidence either to support or refute that account.

What were the lessons of this unusual avalanche of publicity? On the positive side it proved that there was a huge reservoir of worldwide – albeit somewhat anthropomorphic – concern for an animal. Almost certainly, much of this was encouraged by the media and helped by the fact that the animal concerned had a name and was in a situation with which everyone could identify in a personal way. The publicity which showed us to be a caring institution was good for Marwell and by extension the responsible sections of the rest of the zoo world. I could not but reflect, however, that had the same level of care and interest been sustainably directed to the extinction crisis that threatens so many species and habitats on our planet then it would have been of much greater benefit to Giraffe and all other life forms.

On the negative side was the fact that we had lost a fine animal, and among the global interest was an element of rather macabre prurience. The only truly sour note that I recall is of two ladies who asked the gatekeeper on the afternoon of Victor's death if the animal was still alive and who, when told that he was not, complained loudly of the wasted cost of a journey from Salisbury (about 30 miles) and departed without deigning to enter our portals. Many years on, I am constantly accosted by people who say how well and clearly they remember the Victor incident. Almost without exception they are amazed when I tell them how long ago it all was.

The year of Victor's death was a year during which we had given a great deal of thought to the future of Marwell Zoological Park, which was by then sufficiently established as a public attraction for us to feel that it had a long-term future. Margaret and I wanted to ensure that the zoo's existence would not be terminated by my untimely death, with the taxation as well as the personal implications of such an occurrence. Discussions took place between us and my two sons, and with our legal and financial advisers, about donating all, or part, of Marwell to a charitable trust. Through our legal advisers discussions were begun with the Charity Commissioners, the outcome of which was that this could be done if we donated the land within the zoo's perimeter fence and the animals and all therein to a new charity – which represented an enormous loss of a hard-won and, to us, very significant asset. We chose to proceed, and when the creation of the Marwell Preservation Trust was announced some six months after his death, the media's memory of Victor ensured widespread press coverage.

Chapter 9

On 1st March 1978 the Marwell Preservation Trust became the owner of the freehold of Marwell Zoological Park and its animals, together with all the fixtures and fittings, equipment and vehicles necessary for the operation of an already sizeable undertaking.

Students of inflation may be interested to note that in the balance sheet which was included in the new Trust's first annual report (which actually was for only ten months, as we wished future financial years and reports to be on a calendar year basis) the freehold together with animal buildings, fences, plant, vehicles etcetera was shown as just below £573,000. That sum in 2008 would just about purchase a comfortable four-bedroom house in Winchester.

This was still a time when zoos traded animals, and for the new Trust this was a welcome source of income from its inherited successful breeding programmes. The balance sheet valued the animal collection at £171,183, a figure that appeared yearly until 1982 when, in recognition of the growing acceptance of the conservation responsibility of zoos for their wild animals, the figure was reduced to a token £1. An accompanying note in the annual report for that year stated that: 'the Trustees consider an annual valuation of the animal collection to be inappropriate'. For me this statement embraced a philosophy so well articulated by that great German zoo Director and conservationist Bernard Grzimek, who entitled one of his memorable books *Rhinos Belong to Everyone*. Surplus for that first ten months was £104,437 which appeared a little better than it really was as it excluded the first two months of that year, January and February, which are always high in costs and low in income.

I recruited a small group of like-minded people for the initial board of trustees; people that I knew well, and who shared my goals for Marwell and its philosophy. Our first chairman, Tim Walker, was a remarkable man who sadly was to be snatched from us by a cruel death too early in his and our lives. Tim, who came from a naval and military family background, had made himself a considerable fortune as one of the founders of Hambro Life Assurance. Unlike so many who acquire great wealth he chose not to buy large yachts and houses in exotic locations, but to buy and restore to its former glory a fine house with a small estate of 22 acres on the outskirts of Bradford-on-Avon in Wiltshire. There he decided to establish some non-domestic animals as an outdoor counterbalance to the fine furnishings and paintings within.

We had first met some while before the formation of the Marwell Trust as a result of Peter Bircher delivering to him a group of Marwell-bred Blackbuck (an Indian subcontinent antelope species, then as now commonly kept and bred in zoos) which I had sold to the animal dealer Ravensden, who had requested that we made the delivery. Peter returned from this mission impressed by the keenness of their new owner to establish a private animal collection, and his strong advice to me was that I should meet this enthusiast. This I did, and from that first meeting sprang a friendship based on shared passions for animals as well as what for want of a better expression I will call the 'high life'. Tim had apparently endless money to invest in his enthusiasm, and by this time I had a wide circle of contacts in the zoo world through which I was able to help him assemble an impressive private animal collection, of which some animals came from Marwell but many were from sources that for a number of reasons (mostly financial) were beyond my reach. These included Przewalski's horses, Grevy's zebras, and Kulan amongst the equids and Scimitar-horned oryx amongst the antelope as well as a fabulous group of Roan antelope, the most noble of antelopes which later came to Marwell and Whipsnade, and were destined to be the forebears of animals that I would later send to Swaziland. In 1976 Tim had become a trustee of the UK branch of the World Wildlife Fund (WWF) and in 1984 its chairman.

My long-time friend and solicitor Alan Eades was another founder trustee. Led by Alan, then the senior partner, his Norwich-based firm of Mills & Reeve had dealt with the purchase of the Marwell estate and had been the leaders of the legal team in my fight for planning consent. They had dealt with the Charity Commissioners in the establishment of the Trust, and a partner of Alan's, William Barr, was our first Secretary, an office that he filled until after my retirement. However, Alan and I went back to long before my zoological dreams took shape. He had been a director with me of a number of companies related to poultry activities, and we had been together on business to many places including America and Lebanon. Happily we shared an ability to have some after-hours fun whenever our exhausting travels allowed. Until he reached the Trust's mandatory retirement age of 70 (something that I initiated for convenience, but lived to regret) Alan was a continuing source of support and wisdom as well as friendship.

Jane Cole had been a key supporter of the Marwell concept from its very first announcement and, as a Hampshire County Councillor, Chairman of Winchester WWF and WWF (UK) Trustee, her support had been very valuable. Jane's husband Robin was a passionate gliding enthusiast, a sport which brought them both into contact with Sir Peter Scott, one of the early instigators of conservation awareness. Peter made disciples of them both. Jane was made a Knight of the Golden Ark by Prince Bernhard of the Netherlands in recognition of her work for conservation. She and Robin were also passionate about limiting human population growth and gave much support to Population Countdown, a charity dedicated to the encouragement of birth control amongst impoverished peoples. They recognised the interrelationship between the growth in human numbers and aspirations and the loss of wildlife. Individually and through their company's charitable trust they provided much financial help for conservation causes and Marwell was one of the beneficiaries of their generosity. Jane took a particular interest in Marwell's education role and she served on the Education Committee. Until she reached Marwell's mandatory retirement age Jane was another constant strength and support through some very difficult as well as good times.

The wildlife artist David Shepherd, who Margaret and I had first met with Tig at the launch of his fundraising limited edition picture *Tiger Fire*, agreed to be a founding Trustee despite his incredibly crowded diary. Apart from his commitments as one of the world's most successful living artists with a constantly full order book, David is an indefatigable proselytiser and fundraiser for conservation causes, with an irresistibly charismatic speaking style. I have shared a platform with him and felt in every way outclassed! A man of passionate forthrightness, he resigned after four years, no doubt because of the pressures on his time, although he did blame me for deluging him with paperwork. Happily we remain friends and he once welcomed me onto the footplate of his famous steam engine *Black Prince* and allowed me to pull the whistle! Steam engines and the East Somerset Railway where *Black Prince* and other engines lived are his second passion.

At the beginning of my foray into Hampshire I was contacted by a man called John Adams who was then working in his father's engineering consultancy but whose real interest in life was zoos, of which he has an encyclopaedic knowledge. He is a 'zoo buff' through and through. It was John who organised the supporters who came forward in Marwell's first year into the Marwell Zoological Society, of which he became the Secretary. His enthusiasm and knowledge of the zoo world, together with his role with the Society, made him an ideal founding trustee. John continued as a trustee until the overall growth of Marwell activities created a paid role for him, at which time as a salaried person he was no longer eligible for what by law and its very nature must be a voluntary post.

As with solicitor Alan Eades, I also had a long association, from my business days, with an accountancy practice based in Norwich. This, by 1978, had become Peat, Marwick, Mitchell & Co. and it was destined to change its name once more and become KPMG. The senior partner of that practice, Harry Hornor, had long since become a friend as well as financial adviser and was deeply involved in Marwell from the beginning. As the auditor to the Trust Harry was not eligible to be a Trustee, but he attended all our meetings and when he retired became a Trustee until he too reached our 70-year retirement age. When Harry retired from the practice in Norwich, our accounts were taken over by the Southampton branch and our meetings were supported by Mike Killingley, then senior partner of that branch, who in turn became a Trustee when he left accountancy.

I too became a member of the board which, in an unfortunate but then unforeseeable way, was to cost the Trust a slice of VAT repayment after the charitable zoos had won a hard fought battle with HM Customs & Excise. The Charity Commissioners were reluctant for me to be both a Trustee and the paid Director, but were persuaded that because of my role as a founder this was acceptable providing I surrendered all employment rights. In other words a majority of the Board could fire me at any time without compensation. I needed the income, as I had given away most of what I had earned over my lifetime to date. I still had the farmland around the zoo but that was too small an acreage to be profitable, particularly as I had no time to work on it myself. Even at that time 250 acres was barely viable even if it had an owner who could be a full-time worker, so with an owner who was a full-time Director of the neighbouring zoo the farm had little chance of making a profit.

The farm benefited the zoo by providing hay and straw at 'on-farm cost' as well as somewhere to dispose of used animal bedding. Most importantly, by ensuring that no ruminants were kept on land adjacent to the zoo, I provided a cordon sanitaire against risks such as the much feared foot and mouth disease, as well as keeping away any entrepreneurs who might wish to start some enterprise that benefited from proximity to a zoo. Such a one was started on land just beyond my own, and used the Marwell name which was a constant source of confusion to the public and annoyance to our telephone switchboard.

Margaret became a Trustee in 1980. We had felt it important not to create an impression of family domination too early on. Over the ensuing years many fine people came forward to give us their support and time as Board members. I have often been asked why I went to the trouble and expense of forming a new organisation when in the form of the Marwell Zoological Society a suitable charity already existed. The answer is simply that I did not believe that a democratic body (which the Society was from its inception) with a lay electorate was an effective way of guiding and managing a zoo. Later, when for a time I was involved in the affairs of the Zoological Society of London, I became very aware that I had got that one right! Animals quite rightly arouse passions, and if these have to be debated at length by a council, which in turn is responsible to an electorate which is not necessarily in a position to make sound judgements, then progress is at best slowed and at worst stopped.

I have been told that the word 'caucus' is one of the very few truly American words, and means a 'gathering of like-minded people'. It was my wish that the Marwell Board of Trustees should be such a gathering. In this I succeeded for a quarter of a century until I became too trusting of later Board members. The financial benefits of a charitable status are substantial. The most immediate of these was a mandatory forgiveness by Winchester of 50 per cent of local taxes (which were then called rates) and the city then, as a token of its support, forgave us the other half. Income and inheritance taxes were no longer a threat so profits, if any, could be wholly retained and death of the owner would not be a threat to financial survival. As a charity we always referred to profits as either a 'surplus' or, perhaps even more stuffily, 'excess of income over expenditure'.

We were at the beginning overly confident of attracting donations and sponsorship for a menu of needs, but soon learnt that this is by no means an easy task. Ironically, animal welfare charities attract far more support than conservation. I applaud their work but believe that the fundraising disparity is because their message is simpler than ours. I also wonder if conservation is often seen as being rather elitist. Certainly no rush of new funding came our way other than from animal adoptions. This kind of support, whereby a benefactor's donation is linked to either a particular (sometimes named) animal or a member of a species, had been offered in the past but I had always declined it as there was no way that it could be accounted for outside of what could have been regarded as 'Knowles' own money' whilst the zoo was in our personal possession. I have noticed that other zoos have had no such scruples, so I was probably wrong in this view. From 1978 onwards adoptions were a major source of income. Another income source, albeit a long-term one, for any charity is that of legacies, and Marwell was destined to benefit from these in later years. I always told anyone who might be minded to leave us money not to let me know, as ever afterwards I would be unable to greet them with the normal courtesy of 'How are you?'!

In 1979 and 1980 Marwell devised and hosted National Wildlife Fairs to enable ourselves and other conservation charities to have a shop window for our work. With the addition of some fun and commercial activities we attracted substantial audiences, and with the support of famous names like Peter Scott and David Attenborough spread the conservation message very effectively. However the financial experience was shaky, to say the least, and with our then weak financial base we did not feel able to continue the event. The early years of Trust ownership of Marwell were in retrospect amongst my most fulfilling. The zoo was 'established' in the eyes of the local community, whence came the beginnings of financial support and increasing visitor numbers. It was in many ways a time of steady growth, although often too slowly for someone as impatient as myself.

The international zoo community which, thanks to my early American connections had always been supportive, recognised both myself as an individual and Marwell as an institution by admitting me to membership of the prestigious International Union of Directors of Zoological Gardens (IUDZG) at its 1980 annual meeting hosted by Pretoria, the National Zoo of South Africa. Membership then was not easily achieved and newcomers had to give a paper to their peers and were subsequently voted on by them. My good friend Jeremy Mallinson, then the Director of Gerald Durrell's famous Jersey Zoo, was also 'up for election' that year and we were both made a little nervous as our British colleagues impressed on us that, should we stumble, there would be great damage to national pride as only once in the history of the Union had someone been refused membership as a result of his paper. That unfortunate person was an Englishman! Happily we both made it, and both of us enjoyed annual meetings in many locations until our retirements. These were hosted mostly by large zoos which had the administrative infrastructures for a substantial organisational commitment. Every meeting that I recall was pleasurable, with a substantial social component, including a spouses' programme, but also with the major benefit of opportunities to see other zoos from close to, and to network with a group of people with whom one shared passions and challenges.

Inevitably the Union changed over the years of my membership as many of us became increasingly aware of our awesome responsibilities to conservation and a need to add more seriousness to some of our debates. I recall being taken to one side by a long-standing member, the Director of one of the major German zoos, who began by telling me that he liked me personally, but felt that I should know that in earlier days membership of the IUDZG was like belonging to a rather splendid Rotary International club, but then along came people like myself who introduced serious matters and rather spoilt things! Necessarily the 'serious side' prevailed and the IUDZG became the World Association of Zoos & Aquariums (WAZA) with its own paid Directorate and a less restrictive but more democratic membership base which included national zoo associations as well as individual zoos.

Fortunately, retired zoo directors (which include those with flashier titles such as President or Chief Operating Officer) are made honorary members and allowed attendance at meetings as well as receipt of all publications. I attended two meetings as an honorary member, one in Vienna and one in New York, and found both to be more businesslike than in earlier days but equally enjoyable.

However, it was always the animals that gave me my real fulfilment, and throughout my directorship the collection grew both in numbers of individuals and species. Earlier I have mentioned that female births are always hoped for with herd animals. In the Trust's first year another of my favourites, the Ellipsen waterbuck, provided nine male calves in a row!

Quite early in the Trust's time we enjoyed close cooperation with London Zoo where we quarantined ruminants from European zoos. This enabled the foundation herd of Sable antelope to be strengthened in 1978 by three females and a herd of Congo buffaloes to be acquired, in joint ownership with Tim Walker. Never common in zoos, they are smaller cousins of the better-known and much more aggressive African buffalo, which is often referred to as the Cape buffalo. Not only are they smaller but they are of a predominantly orange hair colouring and have hairy ears, which I suppose had an evolutionary purpose of keeping out insects in the humid areas of West Africa to which they are native. These are the very areas where the present-day bush meat trade is flourishing in association with forestry, and which represents a threat to this subspecies. I am often asked which my favourite animals are. This is a question that I find almost impossible to answer as I truly find all life forms intriguing, but if forced to provide an answer these hairy-eared smaller cousins of one of Africa's 'Big Five' would certainly be on the list.

By 1982, after lobbying by the Zoological Society of London and ourselves, we were regarded by the British veterinary authorities as being sufficiently trustworthy to be allowed to have our own quarantine in buildings at a port of entry, which was first at Southampton docks where our building staff converted unused buildings for the purpose (and eventually dismantled them). At that time British dock workers were very militant and our builders were told that our requirements could only be carried out by registered dock labour. An explanation by me of the reasons for our work and our poverty, combined with a judicious distribution of free tickets, overcame that little local difficulty. For a number of years we continued to use dock areas for the quarantine of imported ruminants at Southampton and later at Poole, which enabled us to establish the significant groups of African antelope for which Marwell became famous. In later years it became possible for zoo-to-zoo imports to be achieved, with suitable disease testing and reams of paperwork, from within the European Community.

Once the property which included Marwell Hall passed into the new Trust's ownership, Margaret and I were no longer homeowners, and it seemed prudent to find a home of our own. This was no easy task as in those days I was still (usually happily) committed to curatorial duties and needed to be within no more than ten minutes' drive of the Park and preferably within radio range. Anyone who has house-hunted within that kind of limitation in addition to their own preferences will know how frustrating a process this can be. In our case it took just on two years to find somewhere that met all our criteria, but we finally succeeded and in March of 1980 we relinquished occupation of the rather grand but totally impractical white elephant in the middle of the zoo.

Apart from wishing to have a long-term home of our own, there were a number of reasons for feeling that the time had come to move out. Living over the shop, no matter how much we loved it, restricted both our privacy and our peace of mind. I simply could not avoid hearing something unusual taking place in the offices below our living area or seeing unexpected activity through windows which gave us views of much of the Park itself. To have a relaxing day and recharge our batteries we always had to get in a car and drive away somewhere. In much of the winter the large rooms were seriously cold as the ancient central heating was, to say the least, inadequate, and when a radiator ceased to work we were advised to do nothing as any attempt to undo the pipework, which was very old and thin, might precipitate a crisis of unimaginable proportions. One harsh winter night will be forever memorable. Before retiring we went to the giraffe house to get warm, as there was no way that those creatures could be expected to endure our level of discomfort. We just stood in the public area huddled together in our many layers of clothing whilst being looked down on by creatures puzzled at these surprising intruders soaking up the warmth. The following morning our bedside water glasses were frozen despite electric heaters battling the chill. There simply was not the money available to divert from the zoo's many needs to domestic comfort.

Roo, our hand-reared Bennett's wallaby, came with us when we moved, and of course she could not live on her own so a small group of her species was established in a fox-proof paddock where I also established my groups of bantams, which had long been an interest of mine. Perhaps I could never totally get the chicken feathers out of my blood! As our property had a public footpath across it news soon spread that Knowles was starting another zoo – this time without planning permission! The short-term accommodation of two Sarus cranes for which the zoo had no room at the time helped feed that rumour.

Amongst the wallabies we had an albino male which was consistent with a money-making policy that I had instituted at the zoo a few years earlier. Princess Elizabeth had been given a pair of these albinos when, during a visit to Australia, she visited Sydney's Taronga Park Zoo. This was at a time when gifts of exotic animals to heads of state were frequent, and in Britain's case these were all passed on to the Zoological Society of London, which placed the wallabies in Whipsnade. Their albinism came from a recessive gene which meant that an albino male mated to a normal-coloured female produced normal-looking offspring which however carried this recessive gene, and would if mated to another recessive carrier produce albino offspring. There was a demand for these unusual animals in America which I then unashamedly exploited for the benefit of Marwell's finances. Roo, although often seen mating, never produced a baby. I suspect that as is the way with marsupials she may have produced the tiny

112

foetus-like animal that finds its way to a mother's pouch, but being hand-reared she lacked the instinct to assist this passage and discarded the tiny strange naked little object which had appeared in her life.

Once we had moved out of Marwell Hall it became more important that this hitherto white elephant and its surrounding grounds started to contribute to the aspirations that we had for Marwell. During 1982 building work was started so that the garden areas at the rear of the Hall could be made available to the public. Attractive south-facing houses and enclosures for small South American primates were built against an ancient brick wall and near an arbour where one legend has it that Henry VIII first proposed to Jane Seymour, whose family had been given the large Marwell estates of that time. These buildings were in keeping with that historic area. Fortunately that work was completed before the Hall was given a Grade I listing following an inspection of the property by the Historic Buildings Bureau of Hampshire County Council. Although this was something of a mixed blessing, without it the noble Hall would not be standing today.

The Grade I listing opened the door for grants from English Heritage to preserve the building, and after two years of form-filling and correspondence, all was agreed and work commenced in 1987 and continued for several years thereafter. Both Winchester City Council and Hampshire County Council promised contributions. However, in spite of this our white elephant was a financial drain for several years. Most of the work was sensible and achieved the desired result of securing our piece of history for the foreseeable future. One condition which I disputed, but lost the argument, concerned what was grandly referred to as the porte-cochère which is a flat-roofed covered area by the front door through which in olden days a horse-drawn coach would have been driven to ensure that its passengers could alight with as little exposure to the elements as possible. The architecture of the Hall is such that the only possible way to view this flat roof is to climb a ladder and peer over the faux battlements. It is not overlooked by any window. Our architect (Mrs Corinne Bennett, who at that time was responsible for Winchester Cathedral) suggested that this should be made waterproof with stainless steel sheets properly laid, but our grant-givers insisted on the use of the original material, which was lead, at a cost of an extra £10,000.

Apart from its long history and association with the family of Henry VIII's favourite wife, Jane Seymour, and the weakly son that she bore him, the Hall was considered important because the original roof structure, still intact below the more recent one, was considered to be almost unique. One very hot summer's day a Canadian lady, of rugby prop forward proportions, was introduced to me as a world authority on medieval roof structures who would like to inspect our treasure. When she returned from this, covered in sweat and cobwebs, she sat down in my office and without any preliminaries slapped a bare but substantial thigh and declared that I had the finest medieval crutch that she had ever seen!

The early 1980s were yet another troubled period in the economic history of post-war Britain and tight family budgets and unemployment impacted on visitor income both from gate takings and from retail and catering sales. The proverbial ill wind did, however, at this time blow us some good. Education is one of the important roles of a zoo. Our animals are not, as in former times, curiosities to be gawped at, but ambassadors for their kind and the areas of our planet to which they are native. From Marwell's very beginning, endangered species' enclosures had a black sign with an emblematic skull on it with words indicating their status. Staff (whose feedback of visitor comments was always of great value to me) frequently reported that visitors often exclaimed that they had no idea that so many animals were at risk.

Clearly, signage designed to attract attention was in itself educational, but I had always known that we should go much further and offer more formal education, particularly to the younger people who are destined to inherit the world bequeathed to them by the generations that are its temporary custodians. Marwell needed education staff and a building in which to give lessons to at least some of the 30,000–40,000 school children who by this time were visiting annually. It was to meet this need that the 'ill wind' blew our way and did good, for in 1981 the Trust signed an agreement with the Manpower Services Commission (MSC) for a Community Enterprise Project which provided us with two teachers and a graphics artist so we could establish an Education Centre in the recently vacated Hall. Their modest salaries were paid by the taxpayer together with a sum of money to the Trust to help meet our costs.

The rooms available were not ideal, but from the beginning we and the visiting children had the benefit of highly motivated people who were brilliant at the art of making silk purses from sows' ears. The scheme was so successful that in its second year there were two full-time and three part-time teachers. The teaching staff were supported by two part-time graphics artists, a part-time handyman and an administrator. I would rate this as one of the most successful of government initiatives, not only for Marwell but also for many of the people who benefited from a working environment which not only gave them an opportunity to develop their own abilities but exposed them to the world of wildlife conservation at the heart of the zoo. Many who left us succeeded in related fields using knowledge and contacts developed whilst with us. One from those early days, Clare Sulston, stayed until long after my retirement. For a time she was head of the department, only relinquishing that post when starting a family.

Hampshire Education Authority (HEA) soon recognised the importance of Marwell's contribution to the young people of the county. In 1985 a formal relationship was established which included funding by the HEA for a head of department, in return for which financial concessions were granted to visits by Hampshire school children, and an advisory committee was established which included HEA representatives. The following year further support was given and another permanent, part-time post was created. Despite this help the department remained very dependent on the MSC to provide the level of staffing necessary for the quality service which we were determined to maintain, so the loss of funding when the MSC scheme closed in 1988 was a cause of serious concern until, happily, the HEA again came up trumps and agreed to fund sufficient teaching staff for the 1988 season.

My philosophy, supported by the Trustees, was that zoo-based education was so important a part of our mission that it should not be required to produce a surplus, but equally should not be a financial drain on the rest of our activities. With the HEA help this was achieved. Thus a first-rate education department which grew in quality and student numbers year by year was maintained by Marwell and the forward-thinking HEA. Local authority reorganisation which separated

Southampton and Portsmouth from the rest of Hampshire threatened to reduce our grants, but lobbying by myself and the chairman eventually achieved a satisfactory level of input from these two large areas of our 'constituency', enabling the forward progress of education to continue. The department and its animals (a variety of small rodents, reptiles, amphibians and invertebrates which were used as educational 'props') merited proper accommodation which they were not to have until later in this story. Until then they had to withstand an annual great inconvenience as we sought to make our white elephant contribute further to our income with another initiative.

It is obvious that the British winter months are not ideal for zoo visits other than by fanatics like myself (I once had Whipsnade to myself in a snowstorm) so there is little income during the season of greatest cost. I cannot remember how it was conceived but somehow the idea of a Winter Wonderland within the Hall was developed and entered into with great enthusiasm by our then General Manager and his assistant, whereby grottos were built and a Father Christmas installed to talk to children and distribute presents. This was, from the start, a quality affair (after all we had space, some of which was otherwise unused, in contrast to shops which could ill afford to surrender money-earning retail areas) with good scenes to be looked at whilst queuing to see Santa, after which there was mulled wine and mince pies for the adults whilst excited children unwrapped presents which had been carefully allocated by sex and age and designated on the prepaid tickets which accompanied families throughout their visit.

Although it entailed an enormous amount of work and organisation and restricted the Education Department for many weeks, it was an enormous success and for many years grew in visitor numbers to the extent that we had to have two Santas (all Marwell Zoological Society volunteers) working simultaneously with a layout designed to disguise this little deceit. Its success was due to the hard work and innovative talents of Marwell staff members, and the enthusiastic work of ever more volunteers who, with constant good humour, dressed smartly and looked after visitors, and dealt courteously with a few of these who, singularly lacking in Yuletide spirit, complained about almost everything that they could think of. We even had complaints about girls being given dolls. This was Marwell being sexist!

I have to confess that one person who lacked the proper wonderful festive spirit was me. I have never been a 'Christmas person' and the sound of Bing Crosby's 'White Christmas' wafting up the stairs to my office from October onwards gave me no joy. Nevertheless Winter Wonderland was a nice little earner at a time of great need and I went along with it until too many copycat Christmas attractions in the area made ours no longer worth the heavy demands on staff time and the disruption of the whole organisation. My successors were spared my torment!

Chapter 10

There is so much more to the development of a zoological park than the assembling of groups of animals and providing for their care. Many skills are called for, including those of a business nature. If I dwell too much on money in this story it is because it was such a factor in my own and my dream's survival and fulfilment. Apart from the animals, the development of the whole complex was a fascinating and largely enjoyable process.

For much of the time after the pre-opening burst I expanded the park gently without troubling the Winchester planning office, until one of our enemies from the original Stop Marwell group of people reported a development which brought the planners' wrath onto my head. From then on every step had to suffer the delays and high costs of planning applications. As we had a hard-won consent for a zoological park, I felt – and still feel – that this was an unnecessary imposition. After all, planners do not know the needs of wild animals and no way were we likely to do anything which would detract from the heritage which we were creating. Apart from our own commitment we had the judgement of those who provided our income (i.e. the visiting public) to consider. As a compromise I established a planning subcommittee to which Winchester appointed a representative from the planning department to act as a liaison officer. This worked very well until that very helpful person was made redundant during one of the times when local authority budgets were being trimmed and he was never replaced.

An example of the kind of frustrations which I experienced was when we sought permission to build the present-day excellent lemur complex in the former kitchen garden of the Hall. Because of the building's Grade I listing, the adjacent areas (the curtilage) needed a special consent, so the planning officer concerned with historic buildings came to look at the site. He was a splendid man, but wholly preoccupied with preserving history. I shall never forget standing with him looking at the proposed site for the wonderful primitive primates of Madagascar, when he turned to me and said: 'It would be much nicer if this could be maintained as a kitchen garden.' I was forced to remark (I hope not too unkindly for he was a man I liked and respected) that kitchen gardens were neither endangered nor likely to be of interest to zoo visitors.

Early in my acquaintance with Edinburgh Zoo I learnt that they had a large hotel in their grounds which provided an annual rent and improved car parking for the zoo as well as itself. Both zoo and hotel enjoyed a bonus of some virtually captive visitors. 'Why not at Marwell?' I thought. Once more calling on the stalwart services of Jim Benham, he and I began another long-drawn-out dialogue with Winchester's planning department. Whilst initially the planners were dubious about the viability of a hotel in such a rural setting, we eventually persuaded them that the location was ideal and the benefit of a hotel with plenty of visitor car parking space outweighed the disadvantage of distance from urban areas. After much dialogue, outline planning permission was received and we then sought a buyer. After abortive discussions with a number of 'wanabees', a deal was struck with a hotel group then growing on the back of a favourable government funding scheme. This group, Resort Hotels (later to disappear into bankruptcy) appointed an architect who designed a hotel which was very sympathetic to its woodland setting and the African ambience of Marwell, and detailed planning consent was granted in April 1988 after a certain amount of haggling over the position of a water tower. Fortunately, in view of Resort Hotels' later difficulties, we sold them a freehold site rather than a lease. When I told our bank manager this news he remarked: 'Now you can lend us money instead of the other way round.' I was very happy to confirm that this was the way it would be. Anyone who has lived for years with a worryingly oversized overdraft will know how I felt!

The hotel itself went through several owners and managers before being acquired by a local family who also own a nearby golf course and who have bestowed on it the love and care which was the intention of the original developers. I never knew what ended the existence of Resort Hotels, but was disappointed to learn that the Managing Director, with whom I had developed a good working relationship, and who enthused about Snow leopards (an adoption was the tangible expression of enthusiasm), was found guilty of fraud and became a guest of Her Majesty. The man had style, for I read some time later that when moved from one prison to another he sent out 2,000 change-of-address cards!

Apart from the costs and delays which planning applications involved, I have no complaints about the well-intentioned staff that I dealt with over the years. The trick I found was always to explain what a zoo is really about and just occasionally to work on the principle that what the eye does not see the rule books will not grieve over! One occasion when this principle did not work for me was with the car park. A zoo like Marwell, set in a rural location away from main bus routes, and beyond walking distance for all but a small handful of people, is dependent on motor vehicles to bring the financial life blood of visitors to its gates. Our original car park was carved out of second-growth woodland and designed so that trees shielded the sight of parked cars from the neighbourhood. We soon found on peak days (bank and summer holidays) that the facility was too small for the number of visitors. Requests to bite a little further into our own woodland were denied, so I instigated a little judicious expansion at the edges of that first parking area. To my chagrin and fury this brought a tree preservation order onto my head. The peak day problem was unsatisfactorily solved by establishing an overflow parking area on adjoining grassland. How I wished the planners were available on days when we used this so that they could explain to irritated visitors why their long walk to the entrance was necessary!

Earlier I mentioned the necessity of allowing visitors to bring their own cars into the Park and the problems that this caused. Long-term solutions were planned for whenever finance was available and the first of these to come to fruition was the provision of a track train. This was inaugurated by the Princess Royal on 23rd June 1987 on what was to be the first of her numerous visits. On that occasion her enormous stock of 'no nonsense' came to the fore. It so happened that we had decided that the engine should have a proper name and that should be *Princess Anne* so a nameplate was commissioned and on the occasion was in its proper place. However, days before the event the Queen let it be known that her daughter was to be known as the Princess Royal. I apologised for our imitation steam engine bearing the outdated title and said that we would be bringing it up to date. Her Royal Highness gave me one of her delightful smiles and told me not to waste the Trust's money doing that!

The railway was named Marwell's Wonderful Railway (MWR), after the Bristolian nickname of 'God's Wonderful Railway' given to their pre-nationalisation Great Western Railway. In order to conform with the wish of the Government Inspector of Light Railways that the engine should always be in a 'pulling mode' I decided to expand the route of the MWR and have two large loops at either end, as the alternative of a turntable would be time-consuming and cause a loss of revenue from waiting eager would-be fare-paying passengers. One loop near the entrance encircled the already established waterfowl pond, but at the other end something new was called for. A railway encircling an uninhabited piece of ground would be pointless. My solution to the problem was a moat inside the loop, on the far side of which would be an island for our Sulawesi macaques who would have a house, accessed by a bridge, adjacent to a passenger station. I think of that development as inspirational. It was designed and created in my old-fashioned way of doing things, without expensive consultants, and it has been a great success for animals and for visitors who are able to view these ever-active social animals with minimal visual obstruction.

My near obsession with Okapi and the fact that I had, rightly as it happened, turned down an earlier opportunity to have one at Marwell has already been mentioned. For many years I thought that there would not be any possibility for me to have such a wondrous animal in my care, but the zoo world was changing and the concept of ownership of animals was giving way to a concept of custodianship. A leader in this changing climate of change was my already mentioned good friend Dick van Dam, then Director of Rotterdam Zoo, who during his presidency of the IUDZG signalled this change during an address which included the words: 'I give Rotterdam's Okapis to the world.' At that time Rotterdam and Antwerp Zoos were the main European keepers of Okapi. Dick's words indicated to me that there would be something like a club of zoos privileged to hold these almost mythical animals, so I set about gently and diplomatically seeking to become a member.

With hindsight, I can see that our first Okapi was sent to us in order to try both our skills and our dedication. A male called Papyrus, who had been born in Paris in 1975, arrived in August 1984, having previously sojourned in Rotterdam, London and Bristol. Of a slightly effeminate appearance, his health was poor and he was a constant source of anxiety to our staff and veterinarians. Early in his time with us I remember discussing him with Peter Bircher and saying that should he die then we would have no chance of being admitted to the club. Peter protested that this was not fair, to which my bad-tempered reply was: 'Who ever said anything in the world was fair?' Happily Papyrus survived for six years, finally succumbing in December of 1990, by which time we were 'accepted' and were able to become a breeding member of a small but expanding group of zoos that are custodians of an animal that was amongst the last large African mammals to be recognised by science and whose status in the remote Ituri forest of the former Belgian Congo, now the Democratic Republic of Congo (DRC), is not well understood. The DRC, like many present-day African countries, is deeply troubled and not easily accessible for wildlife studies and conservation.

My pride in Marwell becoming an Okapi owner together with our improving finances enabled me to embark on one of our largest animal housing projects since the Park had opened, which was a complex of two large buildings each with a number of internal stalls, rather like those for horse stables, and with a wide passage providing indoor viewing for visitors. One house was for Okapi, and the second for another forest-dwelling species, Bongo. We were building up a herd of descendants of Bongo from the Aberdares in Kenya, where the species was known to be in decline. It was always my intention that eventually the Bongo would share another house with the Congo buffalo and Okapis would reside in both houses. Happily that house was built, with design input from myself, before I ceased my involvement with Marwell, and this together with the Into Africa

123

complex on the expanded site of the original Giraffe house became an area of great interest for visitors, both having indoor viewing facilities in which smaller species and outstanding graphics from the Education Department combined to give an African ambience. And those magical, mystical Okapis have two houses.

The earlier construction of the Okapi 'palaces' gave me great pleasure but also some headaches. An architect had dealt with obtaining planning permission and drawing plans to my specification. The houses themselves were prefabricated wooden structures of pleasing appearance to be erected by the manufacturers. I was very happy when the day came to welcome the erection crew onto the site. I was much less happy when a few hours later the site foreman demanded my presence so that he could show me the great problem that he was facing. No one had considered the gradient on which the houses were to be built. There was no way that he could continue unless many lorry-loads of soil were excavated and taken off the site. This would mean a huge disruption for visitors as lorries carried this soil out of the Park, and an expense which could not be funded. Without consulting anyone, I came up with a solution worthy (I think!) of that creator of many famous English landscapes 'Capability' Brown, and had the soil placed nearby in such a way as to create a raised walkway for visitors to view paddocks, both new and already established, containing a number of African animals.

The provision of the stable-like individual pens for the Okapi should have been easy. All that I asked of the specialist company that provided these was that there should be two sliding doors between each pen that had no obstacles at head or feet level that could damage an animal if it made a sudden dash for any reason. It was incredible how difficult these simple needs proved to be. The folk involved with this part of the work were mentally programmed to think only of domestic horses. Not for the first time I was made aware of how far most humans are from understanding non-domestic animals.

One of my many colleagues in the zoo world who became a friend is a remarkably successful breeder of a wide range of animals both wild and domestic. Christopher Marler, more than anyone I know, has an understanding of animal behavioural needs coupled with an eye for which individuals are the likeliest best producers of future generations. He has won every major prize with three British breeds of beef cattle for which he is also a noted judge. For many years he had a bird garden which for a time was open to visitors where he bred a great number of species, including many that are widely regarded as being very difficult. His enthusiasm ran to domestic poultry including waterfowl. Through Christopher's friendship I had a wonderful opportunity to participate in an exciting zoo project in Australia which, although destined to end in disappointment, was to lead me and Marwell into conservation in Africa. His impressive collection of rare breeds of full-size chickens and bantams had been responsible for his meeting with Lord McAlpine of West Green who was then establishing a poultry collection of his own. Lord McAlpine (Alistair), a man of wide interests and enthusiasms, was fortunate to have been born into sufficient wealth to indulge all of these, even if sometimes they were of short duration. His family's firm is the vast construction company whose name he bears.

In May of 1986 Christopher phoned me and said that he had a friend, a wealthy peer, who was developing a bird garden in Western Australia which he was minded to expand into a public zoo, and he asked if he could bring him down to meet me and see Marwell. I was happy to accommodate this request because a day with Christopher's enthusiastic enjoyment of animals was always a delight, and so a few days later I cleared a part of the car park and stood by to receive the helicopter bringing Christopher and Alistair on a visit that was destined to have an impact on my life for an exciting half decade. For Alistair this first visit to Marwell was a revelation and almost immediately he wanted a zoo like Marwell established in the near-tropical town of Broome in the northern part of Western Australia. Shortly after his Marwell visit he invited me to visit Broome as an adviser. At first I was little hesitant about this but my ever-present eagerness for animal-oriented experiences led me to express mild interest, whilst murmuring something about my wife liking to travel with me, to which the instant response was that it was company policy to include spouses in long trips and as soon as I could be free for the journey two first class round-the-world tickets would be provided to carry us to Perth and then to Broome. I often wondered if Alistair had any idea about what happened in the parts of aircraft behind the first class bulkhead!

Thus it was that arrangements were made for a visit in October of that year to see what was already in being and what developments were possible. Broome itself was then a quiet, unremarkable, small Australian town which had once been famous as a centre of the pearling industry as the oysters from which natural pearls are derived were abundant in the adjacent warm waters. Here the masters of the pearling vessels grew rich and built fine colonial homes for themselves, whilst many of the largely Japanese divers succumbed to the bends. As economically important as the pearls were the shells of the oysters from which was derived the mother-of-pearl so beloved of Victorian gentlemen for waistcoat buttons. When Alistair first came to the town it had been in a decline since the development of imitation oyster shell buttons, and the only tourist attractions were the Japanese cemetery and, on the town green, a rusting decompression chamber donated many years before by an English lady who had been horrified to hear of the cause of the divers' deaths.

Alistair had become enchanted with Broome on an almost accidental visit and bought a near-derelict former pearling master's house and restored it for his own use. Ever the enthusiast, he bought and restored other houses and then under a government scheme acquired land at nearby Cable Beach, adjacent to its magnificent 12 miles of golden sands. With the land, which eventually grew to 150 acres in extent, there was much scope for a breeding centre and so I became involved in planning to populate this zoo with breeding groups of animals, initially from Marwell and other UK zoos. My brief, however, extended far beyond this. Being an island with meat production from domestic ruminants as one of the most important parts of its economy, Australia has (rightly in my opinion) very strict laws preventing the import of any animals likely to bring in diseases to which these are susceptible. Consequently the Australian zoos had very few African ungulates in their collections. Also, the influential mainstream zoos were owned by societies who initially were suspicious of this wealthy English newcomer to the nation's zoo scene. As a Director of a Society zoo which was a member of the IUDZG I was able to establish links with these institutions and enlist their support for Broome and their help in quarantining animals from relatively disease-free Britain. It was understood that eventually descendants of these animals would be available for co-operative Australasian breeding programmes. I went further and arranged with the Orana Park Zoo in New Zealand's South Island that species that I acquired from my friends in American zoos should go there for a generation, with offspring then being available for Broome and thus the whole Australasian zoo community.

On my first visit to Broome I found that a huge investment had been made in a bird breeding house together with some fine aviaries both for Australian and other exotic birds. My mission to establish the credentials of Broome Zoo with the established zoos was not helped by the presence on its staff of a man who had once been convicted of a bird trafficking offence. However, when he succeeded Alistair's first manager (who disappeared under circumstances only spoken of in hushed whispers) his capabilities and willingness to cooperate and learn resulted in these concerns evaporating.

As the zoo developed, adult native trees were established and a raised boardwalk was built from which visitors looked down into the animal enclosures. Initially I was opposed to this for it is my firm belief that looking down on an animal does not give the best view of its size and shape. However, as Alistair pointed out, most days in Broome are very hot, but because the zoo was close to the ocean visitors would be comforted by cooler sea breezes. In this he was right, but a problem arose because someone on a boardwalk could be seen from outside the zoo. At this time Irish Republican Army activities were a threat to Alistair who was treasurer of the British Conservative Party and a close friend of Margaret Thatcher. There were therefore reasonable fears that he could be the victim of an assassin with a long-range rifle. Security men therefore patrolled the beach when Alistair might be exposed to this danger.

All went well for some five years. Animals from Marwell and other UK zoos were successfully shipped there after extensive health tests, both before and after shipment, and vast amounts of paperwork and logistic planning. The journeys were in aircraft chartered primarily for racehorse movements to which our animals were added. Often these charters were with distinctly non-mainline operators and one flight was particularly hairy. The aircraft carrying our precious cargo and two Marwell staff members left Stansted Airport and was last seen heading in the wrong direction. When it found Australia it had insufficient fuel with which to reach Sydney and had to land at an Australian Air Force base on three engines.

Throughout the five years of my involvement I took no part in the financial aspects of the zoo. Once when I suggested to Alistair that money could be generated by offering a greater range of refreshments and some souvenirs I was told that my role was to organise the animal collection and not to worry about money. Indeed there seemed to be no need for such worries. No request was denied me or the manager, and when the lease of a 5,000-acre cattle ranch near to Broome was acquired I was encouraged to explore its possibilities for African animals and I brought in consultants to study the suitability of the plants and terrain for Black rhino. This was at the very height of the rhino poaching in Africa and was to lead to my long-term involvement with Zimbabwe. Money, in fact, seemed to be available in a way that never ceased to astonish someone whose first mentor had been a frugal farmer of Scottish origin. Our 1988 planned visit looked as though it would have to be delayed because of a strike by pilots of Ansett, then the only airline that flew into Broome. When I called Alistair he simply said to continue with the original plans as far as Singapore where he would have an executive jet pick us up and take us to Broome, which in fact was nearer to Singapore than Perth, our normal point of arrival in Australia. At Singapore airport we were met as we stepped off our flight from London by two polite uniformed pilots, who had already arranged our luggage transfer, and who then guided us to their waiting aircraft where, after being introduced to the bar and pantry, we were whisked to Broome. After the mandatory rest period the pilots flew to Adelaide, returning two days later with a group of young Ostriches. A few days later they flew us and Alistair to Sydney. It was a lifestyle that we could have got used to!

It was this proximity to Asia which encouraged Alistair to build not only the zoo but also a fabulous hotel on Cable Beach and to develop a plan to build a new airport capable of handling intercontinental planes on the newly acquired ranch. This was to be partly financed by developing the existing airport (which had a limited runway), partly for housing and partly for amenities for the – by now – growing town. I went to a town meeting where these plans were presented to a generally favourable audience although it was pointed out that there were some Aboriginal land claims that would have to be settled. Alistair was very well disposed to the Aboriginal people and at the reception counter in the zoo office a continuing trade was done whereby his authorised staff advanced money to them in return for their primitive carvings – an activity which took a great deal of staff time and soon filled all the available shelves. Ever an entrepreneur, Alistair had a large number of these shipped to England with the idea of starting a fashion and therefore a lucrative demand for these artefacts. This was one fashion that did not take off and on the last shipment of animals from the UK to Broome we had to include two pallets of returning carvings!

By the time of my last visit Broome Zoo was first class. There were fine aviaries filled with many of the fabulous Australian bird species and the spacious well-vegetated paddocks held breeding groups of Greater kudu, Gemsbok, Scimitar-horned oryx, Nyala, Addax, Congo buffalo, Red lechwe and Grevy's zebra, all derived from animals bred in British zoos. Of great interest to me was a group of Marwell-bred Sitatunga, a marsh-living species that is so shy in the wild that in Africa I have only seen a flash of tail and hind legs as one disappears into the reeds, yet in Hampshire in a wet paddock suited for their boat-shaped hooves they are almost tame. For these a large marsh area had been constructed into which they departed from their travelling crates and reverted to their native shyness, almost never being seen again. This happened despite their descent from many generations of zoo-born animals. Opponents of zoos who say that we eliminate the wild characteristics of our charges are mistaken.

During the years of what I now refer to as my 'Australian period' I was in almost daily contact with Alistair's manager, Graham Taylor, who did a very fine job of managing the zoo and his master as well as, sometimes, myself. So it was not unusual for the Marwell switchboard to put him through to me for a discussion. Nearly the last time that happened was for a broken-hearted Graham to give me some of the worst news imaginable. The banks which, unknown to me, had funded our developments as well as a portfolio of properties in Perth, had pulled the plug and he had to dispose of the animals for money, which meant that most of them went to private owners and not the mainstream zoos that I had been encouraged to believe would benefit from our breeding programmes.

It was the end of a wonderful period which had benefited Marwell and other zoos because, as a new zoo, Alistair realised that it was fair that he should compensate us with much-needed money at the beginning of his venture. It was almost like an entry fee to a club. It benefited Margaret and me with luxurious travel to places we might never otherwise have visited, but it was nevertheless a great sadness not to have seen a second great zoo develop with my help. Alistair was always a generous person and although I was never paid for my services I was amply rewarded in many non-financial ways. I am sad, however, that he never contacted me in any way after his instruction to Graham to disperse the animals.

Ten years later Margaret and I attended a WAZA annual meeting hosted by Perth Zoo, after which we flew to Broome to lay the ghosts. We stayed at the still impressive Cable Beach Hotel and had an enjoyable reunion lunch with the veterinary surgeon in the town who had worked so well with us. There was nothing left of the zoo buildings except the animal food store, now a restaurant, where we enjoyed a free dinner in return for sharing our reminiscences.

Chapter 11

The travels in connection with Australia both coincided with and helped initiate a decade of travel closely connected to Marwell's mission and my own belief that (to paraphrase John Donne) 'no zoo should be an island'.

There was a certain irony in the amount of time that I spent in the air because a welcome aspect of my transition from business to creating a zoo had been a reduction of seemingly endless travel. I should not be too ungrateful for that time as it was by the chance encounters of those days that the idea of Marwell was conceived. Also it was two early business journeys to African countries which served to confirm what, as a boy, I must have felt deep in my psyche, which was the magic of the Dark Continent. Then and now it is a place where I feel transformed, becoming a calmer and yet a more stimulated person than when in Europe or America. There was, of course, a difference between my former travels and those of later years. Obviously the latter were related to my true interests, whilst the former were in pursuit of wealth and ambition. Happily I was no longer expected to look smart and could dispense with the white shirt, corporate tie and dark suit. Scruffy is my natural appearance!

Travel itself has changed vastly in the four decades of my story – and not for the better. Back in 1961 long-distance air travellers were not as numerous as they are today. Passengers were not then subjected to the herding that characterises present day journeys. Not for nothing is 'economy' class referred to as 'cattle class'. Economy class in the 1960s was bearable because the planes were smaller and passengers were still made to feel as though they mattered. Amusingly, in retrospect, I was able to obtain free access to the well-appointed lounges of Pan

American Airways by the simple device of telling our freight agent that more of our day-old chick export consignments could travel with that airline if I were to be made a member of their Clipper Club. It was not unusual to send 30,000 chicks to some distant destination, so our business was quite sought after. Shortly after that ultimatum along came a large package of maps and other information together with my membership card and a letter from Pan Am's President in which he stated that he had 'long wished to acknowledge my distinguished contribution to civil aviation'. Was ever 'blackmail' so flatteringly rewarded?

From 1980 onwards, with Marwell established as a Conservation Driven Trust, I travelled to meetings in many parts of the world as part of the global zoo and conservation community, but it was not until the end of that decade that I was able to become more directly involved in what, for convenience, we now call the wild, although how much that state truly exists is a subject for long debates which are not appropriate here. In 1989 I was invited to take part in a study in Niger into the feasibility of reintroductions of zoo-born Addax into the Sahara and Scimitar-horned oryx into the semi-desert on its southern fringes known as the Sahel. Earlier we had sent Scimitars to Tunisia in the northern Sahel (where they had become extinct nearly half a century before), but by this time it was known that their southern cousins were also facing extinction in Niger and the adjacent country of Chad.

I had many times before seen poverty, which is endemic to all African countries, but I was not prepared for that of Southern Niger where driving in the capital Niamey and its outskirts was to be besieged at every stopping point by undernourished and downright starving human beings, many with severe limb and eye problems. Niger is a vast, landlocked country with little in the way of natural resources and yet with a burgeoning human population and once wonderfully diverse fauna which, by the time of my group's visit, was declining both because of the poverty of the human population and the wealthy people from oil-rich countries who liked to hunt the surviving animal populations. Travelling north from the capital we passed through areas of adequate rainfall for food crop cultivation before entering the low rainfall area of the Sahel where meetings were held with regional officials and, further north, with desert nomads with whom we shared in the traditional large bowl of a milk-based drink passed from hand to hand (or more correctly lip to lip) in the meeting circle. In the interest of good manners we all sucked noisily at the contents of the bowl without imbibing too lustily. We were by now in the company of very different people to those near the capital. These were proud and independent people well able to survive in their inhospitable homelands.

Our small team was led by a remarkable Englishman called John Newby who was then with the WWF based in Niamey and who knew the area extremely well. John had closely studied the animals of our interest both in Niger and in Chad, and interestingly John had previously been at Marwell where for the first time he witnessed a Scimitar birth. Our second leader was Alexandra Dixon, then with the Zoological Society of London. Both spoke fluent French which is the European language of Niger, leaving me to regret my indolent schooldays as I sought to follow the discussions. John also spoke the native languages fluently.

Something that emerged strongly in the talks with the dwellers of the desert fringes was that the older men remembered when, in their youth, Scimitars were still to be seen, and that they would welcome their return. Encouraged by these discussions we were delighted to find an area ideal for the establishment of zoo-born Scimitar-horned oryx where they could be monitored prior to a 'soft release'.

It is not always appreciated that although wild animal species that are the offspring of many generations of captive breeding will have retained many survival instincts, they will have no resistance to diseases that are endemic to their traditional homes, as their immune systems will have never been challenged by these. Also they will probably still be aware of dangers from predators but not skilful at avoidance, hence the need for careful evaluation of both kinds of threats as well as food and water availability before a reintroduction can take place. I have already mentioned how quickly Sitatunga shrugged off their calm ways when released into a simulated marshy area in Australia. Another significant and very encouraging observation was made much earlier of the Scimitars when first released into large areas in Tunisia. There they were observed to taste known poisonous plants just once and never return to them. Those of us who have been fortunate enough to work with wild animals ponder forever on what is instinct and what is learned behaviour.

Sadly, in 1990, a follow-up mission, prior to meetings with Nigerien government officials, found the area completely destroyed by overgrazing. We never really knew if this had been deliberate or accidental sabotage. However on that first mission we pressed on in good heart into the Sahara itself where it was believed that a remnant population of that uniquely adapted antelope, the Addax, still existed. The desert scene is seldom as it is portrayed in movies – as infinite shifting sands. In fact we traversed much rock which caused endless punctures to our Land Rovers as a result of which we became very skilled at wheel changing, remembering first to pour some water on the wheel braces and jacks so that they were cool enough to handle, as the daytime temperatures went as high as 50 degrees Celsius. That heat was bearable, as humidity was practically non-existent. We were usually able to find a stunted tree or an overhanging rock to provide shade for a midday two-hour break.

In the heart of the desert we had a Bedouin guide who sat beside John and guided him with hand signals through often (to us) featureless terrain. As evening approached, we stopped and made informal camp with typically British gin and tonics before dinner. On one such evening, we had barely laid out the bottles and glasses when our guide came to tell us that he had found a fairly fresh footprint of an Addax, causing us to abandon our preprandial drinks and try to find the animal. In this we failed, and my only Addax desert photograph is of that footprint. Later we came upon an Addax skeleton. In truth our wildlife sightings were very few. I recall some unusually nervous Ostriches and three Dama gazelles so wary that they were gone before any of us had raised a camera. Hunting was a feature of life in that desert. We also saw small numbers of Dorcas and Red-fronted gazelles.

Although disappointing in terms of animal observations I shall always recall that Saharan trip as one of the great experiences of my life. As the desert nights are cold even in the summer, I was glad of a sleeping bag, but usually too tired to lie in it looking at the stars for more than a very few moments. Wisely, I was warned to move slowly whenever I woke because poisonous snakes and scorpions were sometimes known to seek companionable warmth during the night and were apt to repay hospitality with a poisoned bite when disturbed. I was saddened one morning to find some of this pristine area sullied. As we were a mixed-sex group, I felt it necessary to wander off and find some privacy for my morning ritual. Rounding a marble rock I was horrified to be confronted with a huge pile of rusting lager cans. The planet's most dangerous animal had left its mark!

On a particularly long and hot morning, returning from the northernmost point of our expedition, John asked if we would like an ice cream. I thought at first that he was teasing us in rather bad taste, but not at all. About an hour after John's question we came to the town of Agadez, where in a narrow street that could have been a film set for a Foreign Legion epic, we stopped in front of an Italian ice cream parlour which produced truly first-class delights. Although they were out of stock of my favourite banana flavour this was as welcome as an oasis would be to a traveller whose water supply was exhausted.

The culmination of this and a second zoo-based group's expedition was the meeting with local dignitaries. This was destined to be another memorable, although not productive, occasion. John and Alexandra had assembled a formidable team which included zoo directors and veterinary surgeons from Britain and America, and a Texan ranch owner who, out of passion for the Scimitars, had devoted his land and buildings to careful breeding of the species. Our ranks were strengthened by the founder and chairman of the Conservation Breeding Specialist Group, the redoubtable Ulysses S. Seal (known to a wide circle of friends and admirers as Ulie), a man whose many talents included bringing together people with diverse interests (stakeholders) in a threatened species or a habitat for problem solving. The unfortunate tone of the meeting and its outcome is reflected in the fact that we were kept waiting for nearly an hour before the government party arrived, who then listened to our carefully prepared presentations with scant interest. The last of these was by Ulie, after which he was shocked to be asked by a man in flowing white dress how much milk could be produced by an oryx! Put simply, there was not only no interest in our proposals, there was downright hostility. A rather depressed group gathered at Niamey airport the next day for the flight to Paris and onwards to our various home bases.

The two missions to Niger were unproductive and, to the best of my knowledge, no reintroductions of Scimitars, Addax or other desert or semi-desert antelope species, all of which are thriving in zoos, have taken place in the southern Saharan and Sahelian areas. However, John Newby is leading a largely zoo-funded group which is working for the protection and survival of desert and semi-desert species both north and south of the Sahara, which I believe is receiving increasing interest from the northern range states.

My Australian connection led to my – and Marwell's – greatest African involvement in the 1990s. This began when rhino poaching across much of that continent reached such proportions that extinction of the Black rhino in the wild became a close and frightening prospect. In 1989 when all was going well with the projects in Broome, I met with Tom Foose in Harare with the intention of establishing an Alistair-funded participation in an American-inspired constructive project which would have two benefits for Black rhinos. In return for the transfer of Black rhinos to private and zoo facilities in America and Australia, the recipient institutions would provide a helicopter and helicopter support for anti-poaching work with the Zimbabwean Parks Department. I had worked with Tom before whilst he was with Ulie Seal's Conservation Specialist Breeding Group, and we soon formed a very effective partnership, having meetings with the Zimbabwean government minister responsible for wildlife and senior Park staff members. Tom was assiduous at drafting and redrafting documents for these meetings and communicating back and forward with our financiers whilst I, accompanied by Margaret, took some field trips to assess exactly what was happening in the national parks and the conservancies. These latter were the result of praiseworthy initiatives taken by farmers with adjoining land in various locations who agreed to provide sanctuary for animals translocated from areas where the poacher activity was at its most vicious.

The situation was grim. Once we were flown in a small plane up the Zambezi valley by the chief game warden, Glen Tatham, so we could see how easily the poachers could cross back and forwards from Zambia with their booty. There are many islands in the Zambezi which Glen buzzed at frighteningly low level as they were likely poacher strongholds. Only later did we learn that he had written off several aircraft in previous exploits. This remarkable man was totally dedicated to saving rhinos and had been the first person to carry out what later became the accepted practice of 'shoot to kill' in anti-poaching work across Africa.

Later in 1990 Glen received a sponsorship to visit the Farnborough Airshow. As this event is fairly close to Marwell he stayed with us and we lent him a vehicle. On his first visit to our office, my ever helpful PA, Lynne Stafford, asked Glen how she could help with his plans and needs. Her face when he asked her to fix an appointment with the Duke of Edinburgh in two days' time was a picture of incredulity. It took her a few minutes to sufficiently recover her poise to point out that this was not a realistic request!

Eventually agreements were made, a helicopter was acquired, arrangements made for its fuelling and maintenance and Black rhinos were sent to America and Australia (but not to Broome) where they have thrived and bred. Writing this now makes it sound easy, but of course this was far from the case as endless permits and veterinary tests were needed to capture and transport rhinos. The importation of the helicopter and its operation also gave rise to almost as many problems, all of which were overcome by the ever-industrious and patient Tom.

Although for reasons which I have already recorded, no rhinos ever reached Broome, I was later invited to become a trustee of what began as the International Black Rhino Foundation and which soon became the International Rhino Foundation (IRF). This foundation, almost entirely funded by money from wealthy American sources, became a most effective force for the conservation of the surviving African and three Asian rhino species. I was happy to continue my association with Tom Foose, who became the diligent programme director of the IRF, until his untimely death. Attending the annual meetings was never a hardship as they were mostly held in the luxurious White Oak Conservation Center in northern Florida. Owned by the Howard Gilman Foundation, this estate is the home to the Gilman International Conservation Foundation which itself is a significant force for positive conservation in many parts of the world, including the Democratic Republic of Congo, a most difficult African country, where at Epulu, close to the Ituri Forest, protection of the Okapi is a major project coupled with education and practical help to the native peoples. The grounds of White Oak contain large breeding groups of animals including Okapi, Bongo and Derby eland. Both foundations were established by the late Howard Gilman with money made by three generations. The founder was Howard's grandfather who immigrated at the age of ten to New York from Belarus where he started with a pushcart collecting surplus newspapers for recycling. From this modest start grew a paper pulping corporate colossus – a true 'American Dream' story.

One meeting was held on the ranch of another trustee and major donor, Lee Bass, who has some of the Zimbabwean rhinos breeding on his property. Some of us were flown there from Fort Worth in a company plane which landed on the ranch runway, a half-hour drive from the ranch house where our deliberations took place. Association with these people brought home to me the immensity of wealth possessed by some Americans and the good that they can do with it. Wisely, they usually take care to ensure that their beneficence is well used. I served on the IRF board until 2006 at which time I felt that, as my other connections were ending, I should retire. I was deeply touched that at my last board meeting I was made an honorary trustee, as a result of which I continue to receive information on all rhino species in the wild and in captivity.

During a lull in the Black rhino negotiations in Harare, I flew to Bulawayo to visit the Chipingali Wildlife Orphanage, having met its director, Vivian (Viv) Wilson, earlier at a meeting in Jersey. The orphanage, to all appearances, is a zoo – a name I was told would not be acceptable in former Rhodesia. The 'Orphanage' name was to be fortuitous for Chipingali when, on a visit to Zimbabwe, the late Princess Diana agreed to become its patron, although she did not visit. I suspect that, as she had never to my knowledge expressed interest in animals of any kind, she may well have not realised that this was not a children's orphanage. Whatever the truth of that may have been, when after her death it was announced that large sums of money were available for causes once associated with her name, I suggested to Viv that it might be worth his while to apply for money for an education centre. This he did and received £50,000 which then went a long way in Zimbabwe and with it he built a most impressive facility.

Two things interested me on that first visit to Bulawayo. One was that they had Black rhino deposited by the Parks department which were breeding and had hand-reared calves which were being allowed to wander, at times, in the bush where they could make their own choice of type and amount of browse. An ideal situation, I thought, for nutritional studies. The second aspect that grabbed my attention was the number of small antelope, primarily Duikers, at Chipingali and the fact that Viv had made a major study of Duikers across the whole of Africa, including in some of the politically very difficult West African countries. Smaller antelope were poorly studied in the wild and seldom kept in captivity, and this seemed a niche in which Marwell with its bias to African fauna should fit. Viv made it clear that he needed and would welcome financial support and I was able to arrange some of this in a modest way from both Marwell's Trust and its Society.

Viv and I initially seemed to have a great number of interests in common and, in the course of a few visits to Zimbabwe, we moved to the point where Marwell would fund the creation of a new trust. This would acquire from Viv a property next to Chipingali and, with it, some of the small antelopes and the care of the captive Black rhinos which I was given to understand belonged to the Parks department. The existing buildings on the site would serve as residences for a director and visiting staff and students. In this enterprise I was later joined by Peter Stevens, then the Director of Paignton Zoo, who shared my African enthusiasms and like myself was able to persuade his board that this was something that they should support. Thus, the Marwell Zimbabwe Trust (MZT) was formed with Viv and myself as trustees (later joined by Peter) which initially leased, with an option to purchase, 50 acres to be known as the Dambari Field Station some 15 miles out of Bulawayo on the road to the Beit Bridge crossing into South Africa.

Sadly, relationships with Viv became strained and it was obvious that there were substantial conflicts of interests and goals between us and so he resigned from the board, leaving Peter and myself to move the Trust forward, ably assisted by Verity Bowman as Director. We had been very fortunate to recruit Verity – a person of sterling qualities with dual British and Zimbabwean citizenships and a qualified veterinary nurse. I was sad that we could not work with Viv Wilson. I had several times been in the bush with him and as a naturalist companion I know of none better. He did well from the sale, as Peter and I agreed that we should pay him at the exchange rate prevailing at the time the deal was struck, and not at the much worse one then prevailing. This was of great benefit to him at the time of the actual exchange.

Almost from its beginning the MZT has had to adjust to the downward spiral of Zimbabwe's economy. That a country so well endowed with resources of all kinds should implode in so short a time is hard to believe. However, none of these problems have prevented the Trust from carrying out a great deal of valuable work. Anyone familiar with the ways of Africa will understand that, for a number of unfathomable reasons, the captive Black rhinos never moved from Chipingali to Dambari and so a decision was taken to convert the expensively built rhino house into offices, thus allowing all the other accommodation to meet the growing needs of staff, students and visitors. Fortunately the rate of inflation and shortages of materials made it possible to sell the metal used in the construction of the outside rhino enclosures advantageously, which contributed significantly to paying these costs. For many reasons it was, and is, important that the MZT should not be legally connected with its Marwell parent. It is now a totally Zimbabwean entity with Zimbabwean as well as UK trustees, but with funding coming as grants from Marwell, Paignton and the IRF. The fact that its incoming finances are in hard currency has enabled it to continue its missions. Availability of foreign exchange (constantly referred to as 'Forex') is all important.

Although the plan to keep rhinos on the property was never accomplished, we have been able to do much to help the free-living rhino populations by providing fuel for helicopters and land vehicles in support of necessary translocations and, very importantly, rescuing and treating animals caught in snares which have usually been set for smaller animals by people desperate for food. In this, as with other veterinary work, we have been able to assist and be assisted by a very remarkable human being, a man that I am proud to have been associated with. That man, Chris Foggin, as the head of Zimbabwe's wildlife veterinary department, has used his great skills and capacity for hard work virtually single-handedly to help ensure the survival of both species of rhino despite the chaos around him. The MZT is able to support Chris in the ways that I have mentioned, and in turn as an MZT trustee his guidance and support have been vitally important.

Plans to establish breeding groups of critically endangered species of Duikers never matured as none of these are endemic to Southern Africa, and the troubled situation both in Zimbabwe and in the mostly West African countries where they occur made importation impossible. This has been a great disappointment to me as it is in West Africa that the greatest diversity of Duikers occurs, and it is likely that many of these will become extinct as victims of the rampant trade in bush meat. Most of these species I have only seen in illustrations. How sad that they may only in the future be known from drawings and not well remembered because, sadly, they generally lack the charisma necessary to attract a great amount of attention from conservation supporters. I believe, however, that one day future generations may regret the disappearance of these and many other species and realise that if only there had been some in zoos those unique genes could have been saved.

The only non-endemic Duikers that came with the Trust's purchase from Viv Wilson were three Yellow-backed duikers, a larger and very spectacular species which failed to reproduce. It has, however, been possible to learn much of the biology and behaviours of Grey and Blue duikers, which are both endemic species, by studies of the captive groups at Dambari and fieldwork in the nearby Matopos National Park. The MZT has also been able to carry out studies of Cheetah outside the national parks, where in the past they survived more successfully because they did not have to compete with Lions and Hyenas. This was especially true when there were large farms and ranches whose owners appreciated having some wildlife on their properties and could withstand the loss of a few calves from their large herds. The situation became much less favourable for Cheetah when landholdings were divided into small units with very few domestic animals on each. Cheetah all over Africa are often blamed for the taking of domestic animals, when Leopards are the true culprits. Although the two species are very different physically, this is often not appreciated by native peoples and so another valuable MZT activity is education about basic Cheetah biology and the physical difference between them and Leopards. This is accomplished by production and distribution of leaflets and talks to school groups.

I retired from the chairmanship of the MZT at the March 2004 annual meeting and was succeeded by vice-chairman Peter Stevens. Simon Tonge, who became Director of Paignton Zoo when Peter retired from that role, became vice-chairman. The board he inherited included local members, expert in business and finance, and representation from the local university as well as Dr Chris Foggin. At my retirement from the board in April 2006 they too made me an honorary trustee so, happily, I remain informed of the progress that continues to be made by a valiant small group of people led by a dedicated Director. I am proud to have been able to play a part in conservation in a country with the difficulties of present-day Zimbabwe. Interestingly, although whenever I told someone that I was about to visit our operations there they reacted as though I was going into a war zone, in fact I never once felt threatened other than by problems caused by the economy. In connection with this I recall, with amusement, going to dinner in Bulawayo with Peter. Although this was before inflation became astronomical, we nevertheless needed to borrow a shoe box to carry all the cash needed to pay for a modest meal for two.

The vast continent of Africa contains as great a diversity of landscapes and habitats as it does of flora and fauna. I have been fortunate enough to see many of these. None have quite the beauty of much of Kenya, and in that country the most exciting for me has been the Lewa conservancy in its northern part. I was bound to be enthralled by it because it hosts a quarter of the non-zoo population of another species to which I am passionately committed, the endangered Grevy's zebra. This is the species for the love of which I parted with an expensive but un-needed toy (my Rolls-Royce) in Marwell's early days. Not only are the Grevy's one of our success stories but this is also one for which we assumed great responsibility by maintaining the international studbook which records the data on all captive individuals.

Increasingly, zoos have sought to link their work with species which they keep to the conservation of the same animals in their native habitats, and so I twice visited Lewa with the intention of establishing

142

such a link. Lewa is a delight to the eye. At many points on the road system there are stunning views reminiscent of many classic African movies. Often there are views of acacia trees with their tops trimmed flat by beautifully marked reticulated Giraffe, against a distant background of Mount Kenya and its accompanying mountain range. Fenced, but with a monitored opening which allows for seasonal migrations to the north, Lewa is home to flourishing populations of both rhino species, many antelope species, and Plains as well as Grevy's zebras. Jackal, Hyena, Leopards and Lions are amongst the carnivores.

The presence of Lions highlights one of the difficulties facing conservation. Although Lewa succeeds in raising substantial funds from overseas sources, tourist income is financially important to it and tourists want to see Lions. Lions kill and eat hoofed animals, and have found the Grevy's easier prey than the Plains zebras, which have very effective tight social bonding. To me this is a worrying aspect of much of conservation throughout Africa which is largely dependent on tourist income. This, in turn, is vulnerable to economic and political conditions both in the country itself, as in Zimbabwe, and in the more affluent nations of the developed world.

Lewa was once a cattle ranch but on the initiative and funding of a passionate rhino conservationist, Anna Merz, a rhino sanctuary was created on part of the property. A few years later the owners, the Craig family, turned the entire property into the present-day Lewa Wildlife Conservancy which they run so effectively that they and their staff are constantly called upon to assist the Kenya Wildlife Service with animal translocations and anti-poaching operations. Realising that wildlife will only survive if it is of benefit to humans, Ian Craig, the leader of the Conservancy, has been proactive in the establishment of community-based wildlife tourism to the north of Lewa and the establishment of schools and medical facilities in the Lewa area. I had the privilege of being taken by Ian to a meeting with the tribal elders of a former arid-land grazing and hunting community which he had converted to wildlife tourism. The tribe had built an impressive small lodge for visitors and were able to offer a unique experience to discerning tourists. Happily, I was able to arrange funding from Marwell's Society and the Trust to complete a satisfying link between *in situ* and *ex situ* conservation which I hope will endure.

Chapter 12

A love affair begun in the West in upstate New York led to travel to the East and many places in between. With it all came fascinating experiences, not only with animals, but also into many aspects of change as the Iron Curtain, so long a factor in the post-war world, crumbled. Above all, the story of my love affair with the Przewalski's wild horse is a story of co-operation between committed zoos and zoo folk and an example of how a species has been brought back from the edge of extinction to the point where it can truly be considered genetically and numerically safe in captivity. There are also animals living and breeding in their actual former range.

The 'intellectual' journey was far from smooth as I was by no means the only person that this animal had impassioned. At two international meetings, hosted respectively by Munich Zoo and Marwell, controversy was focused on arguments relating to breeding policies, in relation to the amount of inbreeding and the effect of this on the physical health of individuals. There was no doubt that an inevitable degree of inbreeding, particularly with the 'Munich line' (the two lines are described in Chapter 5) had led to deformities, but by the time of the Marwell meeting policies were in place to overcome these. Sadly, one member of the Dutch Foundation for the Preservation & Protection of the Przewalski's Horse, which had no zoo affiliations, became so incensed at the responses from zoo people to the unjustified criticisms to which they were being subjected that he had a heart attack and was admitted to Southampton Hospital.

The third meeting which I attended was hosted by Leipzig Zoo in May 1990, by which time the numbers of physically robust animals were such that, collectively, we felt secure enough to be seeking to reintroduce animals to former habitat, or to similar areas, where they could flourish with only a minimum of human intervention. Quite apart from the meeting itself, it was an interesting time to be in the former East Germany shortly after its demise. I recall that my hotel room was so stuffy that I opened the window only to be assaulted by the intense smell of inferior motor propulsion fuel all too familiar to those of us who had once travelled behind the Iron Curtain. I had been in Leipzig twice before, on tiger-related business, when it was in thrall to a totalitarian police-type state. Then, despite the difficulties which they worked under, I had been greatly impressed by the zoo staff, led by the Director, Siegfried Seifert, who were doing fine work with their animals in stark and difficult conditions. Since the unification of Germany, Leipzig Zoo has been transformed into a very fine modern institution. The hotel car park revealed that change was already taking place as the two Germanys came together. There were the Mercedes and BMWs of the travellers from the West parked beside the ubiquitous, unreliable and uncomfortable Trabants that the socialist 'idyll' had provided for its more affluent citizens.

In December of the previous year I had travelled to Czechoslovakia with David Jones, then Director of Zoos for the ZSL and a Marwell Trustee, to visit two zoos with which both our institutions had close ties. These were Dvur Kralove and Prague. Whilst enjoying a fine dinner in the mansion at the centre of the former we watched on television the celebrations taking place in Prague's Wenceslas Square as the Communist regime collapsed and democracy was being reborn. Our host, the Director of Dvur Kralove, told us quietly that as he owed his position to his membership of the Communist Party he would soon be replaced. Later in Prague Zoo we met briefly with its Director (it was rumoured that he had been an admiral in the Czech navy) who was clearing his desk. He too had been a political appointee and the one for whom the excellent Professor Zdenek Vesselovsky had been forced out of the zoo by the party machine.

Some of us had already been involved in attempting to find a way for a return to the wild of the Przewalski's. At the 1980 conference, hosted by Marwell (which incidentally was held in Winchester's major hotel as Marwell had yet to be blessed with its present magnificent Education Centre which has a large conference area), I had pulled off

146

something of a coup by having two staff diplomats from the Mongolian Embassy in London join the delegates for the sessions of one day. This led to an invitation to Margaret and me to have dinner with the Mongolian Ambassador in London. Seated at a large table in the embassy we were served a vast goulash, vodka and Mongolian wine by a manservant reminiscent of the sinister servant of Goldfinger in the film of that name. Between mouthfuls I extolled the merits of the Takhi (the name by which Przewalski's horses are known in Mongolia) and the passionate desire of its saviours to restore these animals to the ambassador's country. He listened with great courtesy, but at the end of the evening said: 'What my country most needs, Mr Knowles, is industrialisation.' A few years later I was to learn how much the Mongolian people had hated the Communist yoke under which they had lived for many years, and how happy they were at the collapse of what Ronald Reagan had so appropriately described as the 'evil empire'.

In 1985 I visited Moscow as a member of a delegation funded by two United Nations offshoots – the Food and Agricultural Organization (FAO) and the United Nations Environmental Protection Agency (UNEP). The leader of my delegation was Ulie Seal and the Soviet Union delegation was led by Professor Sokolov, then head of the All Soviet Academy of Science. Ulie brought with him Ollie Ryder, the brilliant geneticist from the San Diego Zoological Society, an expert on feral horses from Arizona, and Ulie's then assistant Tom Foose with whom I was destined in the future to share rhino experiences. There was a delegation from Mongolia itself and from the Askania Nova Institute in the Ukraine which historically had played an important role in the history of the Przewalski's. Jiri Volf, the Przewalski's studbook keeper from Prague Zoo was also present. Seldom have I been at so fruitless a meeting as this turned out to be. The high hopes with which those of us from the West had travelled to Moscow were soon dashed as all the participants from parts of the Soviet Union sought to advance their own agendas, whilst treating the Mongolian delegation with little respect. The officials from the UN agencies were preoccupied with keeping track of our *per diem* expenses! My state of mind was not helped by being billeted in the same gloomy edifice of a 'Stalin legacy' hotel that I had endured for three weeks back in

1964. Unsurprisingly, I found that nothing had changed in the intervening years!

The one redeeming feature of the meeting was making the acquaintance of the Director of the Moscow Zoo, the friendly and extrovert Vladimir Spitsin, with whom I enjoyed two visits to his then rather indifferent institution which was apparently little improved since Tsarist times. I remember sitting in Vladimir's office where he showed me a model of a new zoo and told me that the model was the closest he was ever going to get to being a Director of a new zoo. Happily he was wrong, because I have been told that a zoo-loving mayor of Moscow eventually built that zoo and turned the model into reality. From that zoo visit I have three other memories. The first was the stables for the usually nervous Sable antelope which were down steps into a half-cellar beneath the zoo offices. Amazingly, they had never broken any legs! The second was being taken into a pen with two female Cheetahs with ten cubs between them, living together in unusual total harmony. The third was the one and only time that I have received a gentle embrace from an Octopus. Apparently these animals become very affectionate when kept in an aquarium!

Before the Leipzig meeting there had already been stirrings of real interest in Przewalski's reintroduction programmes, probably triggered by a growing awareness that the captive population of our horses was growing to the point where zoo spaces were becoming stretched and the population was healthy enough to take some risks with potential breeding animals. An opportunity to both provide a home for some animals and to test their ability to adapt from cosseting in zoos to harsher conditions was provided by a passionate French biologist called Claudia Feh, who proposed the establishment of a small breeding herd in the Cevennes National Park in France. I was able to help Claudia obtain some funding for this from WWF France by receiving a delegation at Marwell and making a rather rushed trip to Paris to talk to its council members.

Early in 1990 Marwell was visited by the Mongolian Minister of Nature and Environment Protection together with the secretary to the influential Mongolian Hunters' Association. They expressed a desire to have Przewalski's horses once more in their country and I was invited to lead a delegation to Mongolia to ascertain the feasibility of such a move. A few months later, with great excitement, I arranged to fly from London via Moscow to Ulan Bator, where I would meet my expedition colleagues the following day. Little did I know that once more I was to have a traumatic Moscow sojourn and come close to missing a once-in-a-lifetime experience. My flight was with Aeroflot which was then still in its unreformed Soviet mode. It was so late leaving London that, despite the assurances that I was given by the crew, it arrived in Moscow too late for my onward connection. For several hours I and a few other passengers who had also missed their onward flights were told nothing. I noticed that there were brand new telephones in our part of the building which were equipped to take credit cards, so I thought, well, at least I can somehow get a message to Ulan Bator to explain my non-arrival. However, the phones refused every credit card that I had, so with growing desperation I sought help, only to be told that the sole way of making a call was by using cash. OK, I said, so how do I get some roubles? Obviously from the bureau de change, I was told, but to get to there I would have to go through passport control and as I did not have a visa for Russia there was no way that I could do that! All this filled some of the long hours that it took whilst Aeroflot decided what to do with me and my fellow sufferers. Eventually we were conveyed in an apology of a small bus to what I feel sure was once a prison, to be kept overnight. Again my attempts to make phone calls failed, including to the Moscow Zoo Director who I felt sure would help me if only I could reach him.

My sense of panic was heightened when I learned that I was not going to be able to fly out the next day as I had an Aeroflot ticket and the next day's flight was with Air Mongolia. Clearly the concept of helping a passenger stranded through the fault of the airline was a decadent Western one! I knew that if I missed that flight I would miss the whole tightly organised expedition, so after a very miserable night I made so much fuss that I was allowed back onto another creaking vehicle and conveyed back to the airport, where by further demonstrations of just how mad an Englishman can be, I was allowed to buy a fare to Ulan Bator where I arrived, 24 hours late, to be met by relieved colleagues who thought that I had disappeared from the face of the earth. Reunited, we were soon in an ancient Air Mongolia plane en route to the town of Altai from where we were to begin our long overland journey to Gobi National Park B where the last sightings had been made, some 30 years before, of the animal in whose cause we were travelling.

Our departure the next morning was much delayed whilst various mechanical problems were sorted out on two of the three vehicles in which we were destined to spend much of the next seven days. These were Russian four-wheel drive vehicles which I was told were the Soviet equivalent of the American Jeep. Whilst being exceedingly low in passenger comfort they were mechanically simple, a fact for which we had cause to be grateful when breakdowns occurred as we travelled over mostly rough terrain. One breakdown was a back axle which our drivers fixed with a simple spanner, hammer and rocks of various sizes. As we watched this repair I asked our hosts what equipment they thought that they would need for the reintroduction programme. Almost at the top of the list, as with many conservation wish lists, came a Toyota Land Cruiser. I agreed that it would be wonderfully comfortable to travel in one of those, but had to point out that in the situation that we were then in, such a sophisticated vehicle would be useless without access to a modern workshop and trained mechanics.

We travelled with three Mongolian hosts from the Hunters' Association, one of whom spoke English, and three drivers who also served when needed as cooks and tent erectors. Apart from myself there was our biologist Claudia Feh, Jane Blunden, a slightly eccentric Irish aristocrat who although not professionally involved had been a champion of the Takhi for many years, and a female friend of Jane's who never seemed to be fully focused on the mission. Very fortunately we had with us a young Englishman of massive height who was a student of Mongolian life and spoke the language fluently. He had spent some study time in Inner Mongolia which, although a Chinese satellite, has much in common with the Republic both linguistically and culturally. Both attributes were of inestimable help throughout the mission.

Our first night out was under canvas and I shared a very small tent with our interpreter – so small that his feet had to be outside. We were in a valley which received enough of an early frost during the night that his feet came very close to having frostbite! In the early morning I saw a Marten whose coat was already beginning to assume its winter whiteness. I had slept remarkably well due to a very liberal consumption of Mongolian vodka. Unknown to me, Jane had seen my passport and learnt that it was my 60th birthday, a fact that she communicated to the whole party as we assembled in a (slightly) larger tent for dinner. This precipitated the production of a large store of bottles and an impromptu party of sorts which happily laid the foundations of a spirit of camaraderie which lasted throughout the expedition.

The journey from Altai to the Gobi was through a greatly varied terrain, beginning with plains followed by rock-strewn mountain areas, before reaching the desert itself. There was little to see in the way of wildlife, but on the grassland there were domestic camels, sheep and goats in large numbers. There were also large numbers of domestic horses which I found interesting to study. Being of uniform small horse size (134–146 centimetres at the shoulder) similar to that of the Takhis, many of them had characteristics which suggested a common ancestry. On many there were the zebra-like dark leg markings so characteristic of their wild relatives. Often I observed also the so-called 'mealy nose', a characteristic shared only by the Przewalski's and Britain's Exmoor pony, which is believed to be derived from Europe's last wild equines. As I observed these similarities I remembered that one of the contributing causes to the extinction of the Takhi in its native lands was the habit of wild stallions, when denied by competition from having a harem of their own, of stealing domestic mares, thus engendering the fatal wrath of the horse-loving Mongolian herdsmen. It seemed likely to me that many of the horses that we were passing might be descendants not only of an ancient lineage, but also of more recent nights of errant passion.

These thoughts reminded me of an important consideration for any future release programmes. It would be important to ensure that there would not be Takhi stallions without harems that might seek to steal domestic mares, and also that there should not be roving domestic stallions able to father hybrids, which was the cause of genetic difficulty in the early struggle to save the species. Ideally, the only domestic horses near to Przewalski's herds would be geldings, but whether this would be acceptable to the nomadic herdsmen whose horses are at the centre of their working and recreational lives was yet another question for future resolution.

Our base in the Gobi was a place called (presciently) Takhin Tal where there were some permanent structures as well as the *gers* or yurts in which we were to sleep and eat the first and last of our daily meals. These portable dwellings, constructed of wooden frames covered in felt, provided great comfort, with beds around the walls and a stove for warmth and cooking in the middle. The interiors were brightly painted and at first I had a feeling of really being an adventurer away from the distractions of civilisation. That is, until a generator was started outside and our hosts settled down to watch Mongolian evening television news! What are sometimes euphemistically called 'the facilities' were outside and not designed to attract casual visits.

From this base we set out to explore the immediate region which might be the pre-release site and then, more extensively, we travelled in various directions across the desert examining vegetation types and quantities and water sources. One journey took us close to the border with China where our lunch was served by Mongolian border guards. Our food there and elsewhere was almost always a kind of vast stew of meat, potatoes and other vegetables. The fuel for the open fire which heated the pot was dried camel dung dispensed by the same ungloved hands that fed meat into the simmering pot. No one came to any harm. In our travels we saw two herds of the indigenous Kulan (wild ass). The taxonomy of wild asses across Asia can be very confusing but I believe these to be of the race known as the Gobi dziggetai. These were extremely shy, as were the Goitered gazelles, the other wild ungulate of the region. At one well-watered possible release site we encountered domesticated Yak which were larger than any I had seen in zoos. Remarkably, they were hornless. Whether this was naturally so or not, I was never able to discover.

The time came for the long return journey by road to Altai and by air to Ulan Bator. All of us were excited by the potential that we had seen for the establishment of Przewalski's horses, once more in a part of their historic range. Details were gone over many times, and questions asked for which there were some answers that could only be found by further visits and research. Once in a while the inevitable question of funding cropped up but for the time being it was consigned to the back burner. The flight back to the Mongolian capital was another memorable air travel experience. At the distinctly informal airport, would-be travellers, many with produce to sell at their destination, clustered around the ancient plane with friends and relatives who were seeing them off, all smoking happily whilst the aircraft was being refuelled from an ancient tanker lorry!

On our last day we were taken by limousine some 60 miles from Ulan Bator to a place called Hustain Nuruu, a well-watered summer grazing area where fences were being erected for the planned introduction of Przewalski's horses under the auspices of the Dutch foundation which had been so critical of zoo management. We were told that this was not historic range for Takhis and that pastoralism of domestic animals was close by, despite which it was clear that substantial investment and effort was already being made.

After returning to Marwell I was in much communication with like-minded colleagues who had not been on this expedition, notably Ollie Ryder from San Diego Zoo and Waltraut Zimmerman from Cologne Zoo. They had retraced the steps of our earlier mission when I met with them and our would-be Mongolian partners in Ulan Bator for strategy planning in July 1991. This time my outward journey was uneventful. The return in the company, as far as Moscow, of Waltraut and Ollie was made memorable by a reminder of the still sinister aspects of Russia. Our flight landed in the Siberian town of Irkutsk where we had to go through passport control. This should not have been necessary as we were all going to be in transit when we arrived in Moscow. However we had no choice in the matter and all went smoothly for Waltraut and me, but po-faced officials decided that Ollie's appearance did not match his passport photograph and they threatened to detain him. In my usual insensitive way I told Ollie not to be too concerned as I felt sure that he would be able to get a post in the local zoo. Understandably this was not well received, particularly as the view from the plane's windows of drab buildings and feral dogs around the airport suggested yet another place that might warrant the expression 'armpit of the world'. Eventually, by swearing (untruthfully) on something that satisfied the authorities – that I had known him since birth – my friend was allowed to continue his journey with us.

Unfortunately our plans came to nothing and all the travel and planning work which we had invested in our dream for the Takhi passed out of our hands. Sadly, the world of conservation, like any other sphere of human activity, is subject to intense rivalries. Truth to tell, I have often found it to be more so than that of business. Many contradictory views are truly believed in and passionately held. They are also often intermingled with very large egos. The project at Hustain Nuruu led by the Dutch foundation has, I believe, been very successful with a natural growth in numbers of animals which, as in a zoo situation, will eventually be limited by the amount of range available. The project that my group spent so much time on was taken up by others under the leadership of a foundation which also had commercial links with Mongolia. We had not been able to agree a way forward with the leadership of that group. The latest information that I have on this is in a Prague Zoo publication entitled *Gazella* number 27 in which are the proceedings of a symposium held near Kiev in October 1999. I quote from the English translation of part of a report by the former Przewalski's studbook keeper Jiri Volf:

Prezwalski's horses were gradually transported by airfreight to the Takhin Tal station since the beginning of the nineties. After long term acclimatization, the first herd was temporarily released to the open nature in November 1995 and permanently released in June 1997. Second herd left fences in the presence of the author in June 1998. Albeit the animals had suitable grassland as well as watering places available they repeatedly returned to the acclimatization station. The stronger one of [the] leading stallions gained gradually control over both herds. No significant antagonism against wild asses Dziiggetays was observed. According to present experience the limiting factors of reintroduced Prezwalski's horses are predominantly predators (wolves) and climatic conditions (sandstorms, extreme winters) veterinary-hygienic conditions (auto-infections) and antagonistic relationships (mutual aggression) in the case of individuals in the acclimatization enclosures.

Predation by wolves is also mentioned in a report on the Hustain Nuruu animals. This was a factor which we had always anticipated, although an early experience at Marwell when our herd suffered an incursion by the local foxhound pack had led me to feel somewhat relaxed about this. When this happened the mares had formed a circle with the foals inside and the stallion (Basil) galloped round it trying to kill the hounds.

Although in the end I was not able to realise my ambition for Marwell to be directly involved in the return of the Takhi to that part of its former range where the species had made its last stand, I believe that the visits of the group that I was associated with had a role in establishing the feasibility of the project. I also know that at least one Marwell animal did make the journey to Mongolia. Elsewhere semi-free herds of Przewalski's are established, such as on the Hungarian Puszta. The Przewalski's population in world zoos is now strong numerically and genetically and could, should either need or opportunity arise, populate other parts of the range that the species enjoyed thousands of years ago. Back in Hampshire, bachelor groups of Przewalski's have played an important part in restoring former vegetation and thus the native fauna at a place called Eelmoor Marsh which is part of the property of Farnborough Airport. Unfortunately these animals have to be brought home for a short time every two years because of the noise of the International Airshow held on that site.

Despite the disappointments, I regard my involvement with the Takhi as one of those in which I take great pride.

Chapter 13

My passionate belief in the essential role of zoos as advocates for conservation, with an important role in the survival of non-human species, meant that I was a willing participator in what might in some areas of human activity be called 'industry matters' although I deeply dislike the appellation 'industry' to zoos with a commitment to conservation.

Shortly after Marwell's opening I was elected to the council of the British Zoo Federation and to its Conservation Sub-Committee, which was then being reactivated under the dynamic leadership of Dr Janet Kear of the Wildlife & Wetlands Trust. Some years later, when Janet retired from that role, I succeeded her. From before my time there had been a desire by some of the longer-established zoos for the introduction of some form of licensing to ensure proper standards of animal care and public safety at collections of non-domestic animals open to the public. This was passionately opposed by the more commercial keepers of wild animals and a separate organisation was formed, led by the safari parks which then, with the exception of one at Windsor which was started by the Billy Smart circus family, were operated by the Chipperfield organisation.

There was never any doubt in my mind as to where my sympathies lay. Although I always managed to maintain good relations with practically all members of the highly diverse British zoo community, I was aware long before starting my own zoo that there were far too many animal collections of poor quality and with no mission other than the making of money, and there were many run by people who genuinely liked working with animals but who lacked either or both of the financial and intellectual resources needed to maintain acceptable standards of animal husbandry and informative exhibitry. By using the word 'zoo' these collections damaged all zoos and, as a practical matter, undoubtedly had a negative impact on the choices of leisure visits by thinking people who had suffered bad experiences.

The 1960s, encouraged by a belated post-war growth of affluence and leisure, had seen a proliferation of 'animal attractions' which included a rag-bag of zoos opened under some form of franchise from an entrepreneurial company called Associated Pleasure Parks Ltd, a number of dolphinaria and the phenomenon of the 'drive-through' parks which grew in number and size soon after the launch of the first of these at Longleat in England's southern county of Wiltshire. These last chose to call themselves 'safari parks', a name redolent of African adventure as seen on cinema and television screens, but which is a slight misuse of the Swahili word which means a journey. I remember on my first visit to Kenya being told by a business acquaintance that he was just back from a safari. When I asked him what wildlife he had seen he said 'only clients'!

Sharply differing views about the desirability of any form of control of wild animal exhibitions encouraged the British Government to remain inactive on this matter until the Federation secured Lord Craighton as its chairman. He succeeded in promoting a bill which eventually became the Zoo Licensing Act 1981 which came into force in 1984. Lord Craigton (Jack) struggled valiantly to achieve this. I remember that at one point the struggle looked hopeless when he was told that there was no hope of Government funding for a zoo authority to enforce and administer such a law. At this point I made the suggestion that, rather than lose any prospect of legislation, we should propose, as a second choice, that local authorities should be the licensing authorities, using inspectors drawn from two lists of approved zoo professionals, with the first being zoo directors or curators and the second veterinary surgeons with wild animal experience, such a list to be maintained by the Department of the Environment (later to be renamed the Department for the Environment & Rural Affairs, DEFRA). The precedent for this was the local authorities' responsibility for inspections and licensing of pet shops and riding establishments. This compromise was accepted in principle and one of the many items that I am sad to have mislaid in my life is a copy of the bill with a note of appreciation from Jack himself of my 'deadlock-breaking' idea. He had worked tirelessly to achieve this Act, constantly lobbying MPs and peers, sometimes with support from Federation members at meetings in the Palace of Westminster. At one of these I recall being told by Michael Mates MP that he had two zoos in his Petersfield constituency, one of which, Birdworld at Farnham, was opposed to the concept of the bill and one, Marwell, which was in favour. With a certain forgivable smugness I informed him that Marwell was in his neighbouring constituency of Winchester!

There was much agonising over the wording of the bill. It might at first instance seem obvious what a zoo is, but on close examination we found this not to be so in a legal context. The accepted definition became: 'a place where wild animals are kept for exhibition to which members of the public have access, with or without charge for admission, seven or more days in any period of twelve consecutive months'. This clearly called for dispensations as to size and scope of the 'animal collections', as it could in an extreme interpretation include an aquarium with exotic fish in a doctor's surgery. Some small collections also did not warrant a full-blown inspection as, apart from anything else, the not inconsiderable cost would be crippling to them. Dispensations were agreed and to the best of my knowledge have worked reasonably well, although not always to the satisfaction of animal welfare organisations. One total exemption which I never understood was the 'zoos' which were attached to travelling circuses. I have always suspected that a strong lobby came from those at the time. As far as I am aware, this is now pretty well irrelevant in Britain, as public opinion has led to the almost total disappearance of non-domestic animals in circuses.

It is my view that the Act has, generally speaking, worked very well. It has since been amended to give force to a European Council Directive which deals with the keeping of wild animals in zoos. I became an Inspector which, in the early days of the Act, could be both a revealing and a disturbing experience. In concert with a veterinary surgeon and accompanied by a representative of the relevant local authority and frequently, but quite unnecessarily, that authority's veterinary surgeon, who usually had no concept of wild animal care, one looked at everything from the animals themselves and their health records, to public safety and even the standard of the toilets.

The worst inspection that came my way was at Bognor Regis, a seaside resort on England's south coast. My veterinary colleague for this was Oliver Graham-Jones who had been Britain's first full-time zoo vet at London Zoo. Ollie was man of great wisdom in all matters relating to wild animals, who happily was also blessed with the twin gifts of wit and erudition. We gathered early one morning on a day of heavy and unceasing rain to be confronted first by a circular cage of vast height which I walked towards with great curiosity as to what the inhabitants might be. To my surprise there were only two animals within, one a young Fallow deer and the other a Bennett's wallaby, both sitting on their own little islands of fresh hay, which had clearly been placed there for our benefit, in what otherwise was a barren and muddy space. The rest of the apology for a zoo was not much better and we were informed that the local police force was worried about its two Brown bears which had demonstrated an ability to escape from their small moated space into the nearby nightclub, which was under the same management as the zoo. At the end of our rain-sodden tour, which would have been depressing even on a bright day, we stood outside the caravan which served as the zoo office and asked to see the veterinary records. This gave rise to a certain amount of disquiet on the part of the management, who eventually produced some invoices from a local veterinary practice which were their sole evidence of even basic care.

Thankful to escape the rain and the dispiriting apology for a zoo, we repaired to the council offices with the local officials and looked at the forms which we had to complete. These called for recommendations both mandatory and advisory. We could think of nothing that would save so hopeless a situation and so, after a short discussion, we decided that closure was the only possible recommendation and, as this accorded with the wishes of both the local authority and police, this we did and closure followed soon after. As we parted in the still teeming rain, we recalled the last words attributed to King George V on his deathbed at Sandringham, after being assured by his doctor that he would soon be well enough to go to his favourite watering hole: 'Bugger Bognor.'

This was the only occasion on which my participation in an inspection led to closure. Mostly a good-humoured discussion could lead to management improvements, the need for which often arose from surprising discoveries. One of these was when standing in the feed store of a medium-sized collection, I casually asked if anything other than animal food was ever stored in the fridges and freezers. I was assured: 'Of course not', but, as the general conversation drifted on, almost absent-mindedly I started lifting lids and found to my horror and to the intense embarrassment of the zoo's owner, a dead penguin. Another incident occurred when, as was usual after the physical inspection of a zoo, we inspectors sat with management for a discussion before completing the final paperwork. In this case the zoo, which had a large number of Chimpanzees and other primates, was owned and managed by a local builder. When asked the routine question of where the zoo's pathology was carried out, he happily informed us that he had a close friend in the pathology laboratory of the nearby hospital who did all of this work. The look of horror on the part of my veterinary colleague's face is one of my abiding memories! The possibility for the transmission to humans of zoonoses (animal diseases) was mind-blowing.

Over quite a number of years I was asked to be the zoo inspector for Colchester Zoo, which I had known from its beginnings when I lived in Essex. At the time of its first three-yearly inspection it had recently been bought from its founder Frank Farrar by Dominique Tropeano and his wife. Truth to tell, their purchase, although well sited to attract a large number of visitors, left a great deal to be desired, and it was the duty of inspectors to insist on improvements which in this case called for investments beyond the immediate resources of the new owners. Having faced plenty of tough financial pressures myself, I was very understanding. Not always so were my veterinary inspector colleagues. Some harsh words were exchanged in those early days, but I perceived in the Tropeanos a real will to turn a sow's ear into a silk purse. Improvements were made steadily and then innovations followed, to the point where I now rate Colchester as being among the finest comprehensive animal collections in Europe. Carrying through the modern 'good zoo' philosophy, the Tropeanos are now investing in a wildlife conservation park in South Africa.

Although it is now some time since I was an inspector at Colchester I remember it as becoming the most pleasurable of my Zoo Licensing Act tasks once the first difficulties were surmounted.

The 1980s saw many closures of zoos, particularly of those that had sprung up in the anticipated boom years of two decades before. Many realised that they simply could not meet the standards now expected, exacerbated no doubt by the effects of Britain's all-too-frequent economic woes. The nearest zoo to Marwell was the small one owned by the Chipperfield organisation located on Southampton Common which closed before inspections began.

The zoo world moved forward in many ways during the last decades of the 20th century and, as I look back on those years, I am amazed at the scope of the changes and am proud to feel that I played a part in them. Within the UK change was embraced by a small group of zoo directors who, through the Federation and other less formal relationships, moved forward politically, philosophically and practically in ways that the zoos of other continents followed. There was an irony in this because, financially, we were amongst the poorest in the developed world, with the single exception of the two excellent John Aspinall zoos which were supported by his upmarket gambling casinos. Not only did our income depend on admissions, souvenirs, catering and animal adoptions, but we were obliged to pay VAT on admissions. There were several years when Marwell surrendered more money to HM Customs & Excise than it generated as a surplus. Although able to attract occasional legacies and sponsorships we did not live in a culture of giving such as that which benefited so many of our North American colleagues.

Notwithstanding these handicaps we were pioneers of co-operative breeding programmes, effective animal record keeping and mutual support in many endeavours both nationally and internationally. I count myself fortunate that within the UK I found so many like-minded contemporaries, including David Jones whilst he was with the ZSL, Jeremy Mallinson in Jersey, Roger Wheater in Edinburgh and Peter Stevens in Paignton. Some of the impetus for change came from an unlikely American whose vision and personal dynamism had a profound effect on all our lives and our institutions. Ulysses Seal, already referred to in earlier chapters with me in Moscow and Niger was a southerner

162

who had studied and qualified in both psychology and the chemistry of cancer-related medicine. He was a researcher at the Veteran's Hospital in Minneapolis when he became interested in the genetics of tigers. Ulie quickly became absorbed by the conservation issues affecting the animal kingdom, particularly the role of captive breeding in saving endangered species. A bearded man of massive intellect and imposing physique with a voice of resounding but pleasing timbre, his relationship with zoos soon led to his recognition of our strengths and weaknesses. Amongst the latter was a lack of reliable records of individual animals which could be readily accessed. Then, as now, regional and international studbooks for species were being maintained on a voluntary basis by staff members from institutions with particular interest in a species. Valuable as they were then, and remain (now in ever-increasing numbers), they do not lend themselves to rapid and timely information input and access. The time of which I write (the early 1970s) was early in the age of computers, when their challenging technology was bound to appeal to such a man as Ulie. Based in the then new Minnesota Zoo, Ulie was a founder of two important organisations in which I was destined to play a part. One of these was the International Species Information System (ISIS) which was intended to assist decision-making by the provision of that much-needed accurate and timely information. This was where computers came into the story.

ISIS had a difficult birth and a prolonged struggle for survival under the leadership of its remarkably resilient and dynamic executive director, Nate Flesness. There were many cynics amongst the leaders of the zoo world who were slow to accept the role of computers or the need for accurate records. To make matters worse, for many years there were problems with the software, leading to resistance by staff members in those zoos which embraced the concept. Classification of species and subspecies, an area of constant academic difficulty, was yet one more obstacle to acceptance. Almost inevitably, as ever in the world in which I had chosen to immerse myself, finance was an ongoing battle. Nate was asking zoos, many of whom were themselves locked in a constant battle with their budget limitations, to pay for a service which would develop slowly and be of maximum value only when it had a large number of zoos worldwide placing all their records on the system.

Outside of North America, ISIS was seen as being a child of only that continent's zoo community, whilst in their turn many American zoos saw no reason to contribute core funds to a project which would ultimately benefit other areas. Even when the concept was accepted, zoos were able to choose which of the species in their collections they wished to record and as the charges were on a per individual basis this was financially limiting to ISIS and failed to provide the desired universality of information.

I became a believer in ISIS from its very early days and, despite our limited finances and a certain amount of staff resistance, Marwell was an early subscriber. In time I became a trustee and later vice-chairman. At a meeting in Copenhagen in 1990 when ISIS faced a serious financial crisis (because many zoos were unwilling to place all their animals on the register, limiting their entries to only those that they considered 'important' and thereby failing to provide a viable fee base), I proposed that membership charges should be based on zoo attendances and that this should entitle every member to record all the animals in their collections and have access to all present and future ISIS programmes (of which there were a number awaiting development and funding). I also proposed that ISIS should be governed by a trustee board, not appointed, but elected by the membership, reflecting its international status. These proposals were explained and accepted in principle at the IUDZG meeting which followed.

This precipitated me into the chairmanship in 1992, a role that with my limited understanding of computers was only made possible for me by Nate's efficiency and whose tenacious commitment to ISIS and the zoo world has been truly outstanding. I passed the chairmanship to Willie Labuschagne of Pretoria Zoo in 1997, ahead of my retirement as Marwell's director. I was deeply touched when shortly after that retirement I received, as a 'thank you' for my time in office, a beautiful large framed art photograph of African elephants walking head to tail in such a way that it is nearly impossible to decide how many there are.

Since my time the organisation has continued to grow and has developed a software programme called ZIMS, an acronym for Zoological Information Management System. Significantly, as recognition of its importance, funds for the development of this came from the US Federal Government (US$500,000) with similar substantial support from the National Science Foundation and the Institute of Museum and Library Services, also in the US. A further US$4 million came from 133 members of the worldwide zoological community. These sums indicate how valued this organisation has become after more than three decades of pioneering struggle.

Ulie Seal's second major initiative was the establishment, at the invitation of Sir Peter Scott in the early 1970s, of a specialist group within the International Union for the Conservation of Nature's (IUCN) Species Survival Commission (SSC). Initially named the Captive Breeding Specialist Group (CBSG) and, like ISIS, based in offices in Minnesota Zoo, it rapidly became the 'conservation conscience' of the zoo world with adherents spread throughout that community. From its inception I recognised the need for this independent and intellectually strong body, which had the stature to achieve analysis of species problems and seek solutions in a way that no zoo could do on its own. I was an early supporter and became Ulie's vice-chairman and a member of the organisation's steering group.

There came a time, however, when I realised that if something should happen to remove the leader I would have neither the scientific capability nor the institutional support to continue his work. At a meeting of the organisation's staff and most active supporters held at Minnesota Zoo in November 1993, this was acknowledged and provision was made for an appropriate succession. Fortunately this was not to be needed for 11 years. That meeting is also lodged in my memory as the time when I decided to give up smoking. As a one-time cancer researcher, Ulie was virulently opposed to smoking, so to satisfy my addiction I had to find my way out of the office labyrinth at the zoo and stand in the open air on a loading dock. By late November the daytime temperature in Minneapolis was sub-zero and I began to ask myself what exactly I was doing! Painfully, I quit the habit in early 1994.

One of my functions as vice-chairman was to seek financial support from the zoo community at the annual meetings of the IUDZG which were held back to back with those of the CBSG. This was not always an easy task, but gradually the value of the CBSG was recognised by zoo directors and, depending on the location of these meetings, an ever-increasing number of zoo staff participated in workshops which addressed a wide range of conservation issues. Ulie's early training in psychology had taught him excellent people skills, which he used to great effect in drawing people into debates. As it evolved, these skills were shared with some remarkably bright and enthusiastic people who joined the organisation and themselves learnt the art of facilitating meetings all around the globe which addressed a wide range of species and habitat problems.

As the CBSG evolved so too did the zoo community, and the IUDZG recognised that in its present form it was behind much contemporary thought. When I was elected to membership in 1980 it was a very pleasant although somewhat elitist 'invitation-only' organisation with no permanent secretariat, which met annually in zoos wealthy enough to be hosts. By the early 1990s the need for change was widely recognised and at each meeting there was much agonising as to the future shape of the organisation. At the annual meeting hosted in 1999 by Pretoria, efforts to define the organisation's future shape were making little progress when someone suggested that we invite Ulie to join the meeting as a facilitator. With the inevitable flip charts pinned all around the room, he led us to define our individual views and then to a form of consensus from which, in the following two years, the IUDZG became the inclusive and important World Association of Zoos & Aquariums (WAZA).

Marwell in my time had developed a close relationship with the Zoology Department of Southampton University under the leadership of Professor Norman McLean (who became a Marwell Trustee) and our second jointly organised one-day seminar entitled Species Conservation into the 21st Century was scheduled for May 2002 at the university. At this Ulie was to be the keynote speaker, but shortly before the event I received word that he was seriously ill with cancer and could not attend. His place was taken by Dr Onnie Byers, the long-time senior programme officer with the CBSG who was scheduled to be at the annual meeting of the group's steering committee hosted by Marwell. This meeting became, as Onnie later reported, the first of four meetings of a transition team which Ulie himself had identified much earlier to ensure the continuity of his creation. I was a member of this saddened group.

166

Ulie died early in 2003 and was succeeded as CBSG chairman by Dr Robert Lacy, the influential population geneticist at Chicago's Brookfield Zoo which promised to provide institutional support for him in this role. With Onnie Byers as operational head, Ulie's legacy continues, in his words, 'to make a difference to conservation around the world'. I spoke to Ulie on the telephone before his death, a conversation with which I had much more difficulty than he did. Characteristically he was totally realistic about his situation and happily discussed his medical condition and its prognosis, as well as CBSG matters. Despite having no belief in a hereafter, his courage and passion for all that he believed in left me feeling very humble.

Within the world of zoos and conservation my philosophy and practice had been greatly influenced by Ulie and two other 'gurus'. Like Ulie, both of these are Americans, but unlike him each was the leader of a great American zoo. The zoos themselves became major conservation organisations, with their own staff scientists working 'in the field' and also providing financial support to related conservation issues. By word and deed, both provided inspiration and guidance to our whole zoo community. They are Dr Bill Conway of the World Conservation Society (formerly the New York Zoological Society which grew to its present eminence from its base at the Bronx Zoo) and Dr George Rabb of the Chicago Zoological Society's Brookfield Zoo. I am grateful that all three became both my friends and beneficial influences on my professional life.

I served for a time on the council of the Fauna Preservation Society (of which I had been a member long before Marwell was born), under the chairmanship of Sir Peter Scott and the brilliant guidance of its Secretary, Richard Fitter. In those days it was a relatively small but very effective organisation mostly making small grants to 'pump prime' good conservation initiatives, the merits of which were evaluated by its council. It also published (and still does) a valuable magazine, appropriately named *Oryx*. Founded in 1903 as the Society for the Preservation of the Wild Fauna of the Empire, it is probably the oldest conservation organisation in the world. It has now become much larger and more hands-on and is known as Fauna & Flora International. I am happy still to be a modest supporter.

From my childhood, both the London Regent's Park and Whipsnade

Zoos of the ZSL had warm places in my heart and I was honoured when asked to serve that Society on firstly its Welfare & Husbandry and International Zoo Year Book advisory committees and in 1988 its governing council. Little did I know then how deeply I would become involved in the storms which were then building. By comparison with the major zoos of North America and Western Europe the two zoos of the ZSL had always had a very 'hard row to hoe'. In common with the other British charitably owned zoos, not only did they receive no regular support from government at any level but they were burdened by having to pay the dreaded VAT on all income derived from visitor admissions. Alone amongst British zoos at that time, the ZSL had the advantage of being perceived both as a national institution and being of international importance with a long-standing commitment to zoological science and publications. There was always, however, a dichotomy between its dignified institutional self-perception and the commercial need to sustain its existence.

The Society had, for many of the post-war years, benefited from the fierce leadership of a remarkable scientist called Solly Zuckerman (later to be Sir and then Lord Zuckerman) who, shortly after his arrival in Britain from South Africa, became the Society's research anatomist, a post that he held from 1928 until 1932, after which he held many nationally prestigious posts, the most important of which was that of chief scientific adviser to the British government. He rejoined the Society firstly as council member in 1953 and then as Secretary in 1955. The prestigious post of Secretary, although unpaid, was that of the virtual boss of the Society and during his tenure of that office and subsequently the presidency (to which he succeeded in 1977 on the retirement of Prince Philip and held until 1984), he used his influence with the 'great and the good' to obtain substantial donations to fund most of the post-war modernisation at Regent's Park.

From his position of influence in high places, Lord Zuckerman obtained some short-term government funding for the Institute of Zoology and in 1988 a once-and-for-all capital grant of £10 million, subject to certain stipulations that included the employment of an American named Andy Grant to restore the Society to commercial success. It was at this time of misplaced hope that I joined the council and became exposed to a series of events which eventually confirmed a view that I had developed during my chicken business years, which was that the establishment of complex management and consultative structures is not only a massive waste of time, money and human energy resources, but leads to the dispersal of responsibility and eventual inertia.

Such was destined to be the case with the ZSL's two zoos. A development strategy was produced which, although of some merit, was of no use without significantly greater capital than the final government grant provided, or that could be raised elsewhere. Thus, despite a great amount of jargon about marketing and 'rebranding of image', the fundamental problems grew and the departure of Andy Grant and most of his team left the Society with very large financial problems. The loss in 1989 exceeded £2 million and showed little sign of diminishing in the near future. I was regarded as someone who had created a zoo which was financially self-sustaining and became increasingly involved in attempts at problem-solving. I became a member of what was known as the 'core group' and accompanied the honorary treasurer, Lord Peyton of Yeovil, to a meeting in the Palace of Westminster where he sought to use his influence as a life peer to embarrass John Major's government into providing further financial help. This fell flat when the junior minister with whom we met showed us a document, signed by John Major when he was Financial Secretary to the Treasury, wherein he had made it clear that there was never to be more financial help to the Society.

The international business consultancy McKinsey & Company was brought in on a pro bono basis to solve the problems. The bright young team from that organisation put a great deal of effort into analysing the Society's affairs and I met with them a number of times. Unsurprisingly they told us nothing that we did not already know, i.e. that expenses were too high for the visitor numbers currently being experienced at both zoos. To use the language of the entertainment business, the need was for more 'bums on seats'. I remember a lunch (an excellent meal at Brown's Hotel) hosted by Sir Alfred Shepherd, a highly experienced businessman and former chairman of the vast pharmaceutical company Glaxo Smith Kline, for Lord Peyton and myself where, after a long discussion, Sir Alfred graphically described the situation as a 'busted flush'.

Valiant efforts were made to cut costs with Dr Jo Gipps, then Curator of Animals at Regent's Park, charged with reducing staff numbers and other expenses there, whilst Andrew Forbes, who had been placed in charge of Whipsnade after Andy Grant's dismissal of its long-term curator-in-charge, Victor Manton, carried out a similar function there. It was decided that the five divisions of the ZSL should each have a board of its own and I was asked to form and chair such a board for Whipsnade Wild Animal Park (WWAP), a task to which I agreed both because of my affection for it and because within its animal collection were many species that were the subject of management agreements between Marwell and the ZSL. Shortly after my appointment Andrew Forbes decided to seek his fortune elsewhere, leaving me in the unenviable position of chairing a large operation in my spare time with no chief executive in post. Fortunately I had been able to recruit two other Whipsnade enthusiasts in the persons of Christopher Marler (who we met earlier in this story) and Nigel Martin, the former Director of Chessington Zoo (or World of Adventures as it became). Both had been ZSL Council members and Nigel was also a Marwell Trustee. They gave me tremendous support and after an exhaustive (and exhausting!) series of interviews we appointed Stuart Earley as Director with whom we began the recovery of Whipsnade to financial health.

Somehow during the crisis a freelance film maker named Molly Dineen, making a film for the BBC, was given free rein to film staff at work during the painful (to some) reorganisation. She also filmed some of our core group discussions and it was both amazing and hazardous how quickly her presence was forgotten. She filmed two meetings of the Fellows where, not surprisingly, there was a high level of anger. For many years the Fellows had been quiescent, accepting their privileges and contributing little to the running of the organisation whilst accepting that governance came from a virtually self-perpetuating Council. This ended with the realisation of the danger to the Society and its zoos and there emerged a group of Fellows determined to enforce their views and inflict damage on those that they perceived to have been negligent.

Unfortunately, David Jones, the Director of Zoos during the Andy Grant era, who had a long history of total devotion to the ZSL for which he had worked since he first qualified as a veterinary surgeon, was the target for most of the venom at that meeting. Afterwards he exchanged his role to that of Director of the Conservation Department which was already achieving much under his previously only part-time leadership. When Molly Dineen's film was shown on television, it showed David packing his books in his former office ahead of installing them in his new one, followed by a sequence in a taxi as he left for a meeting elsewhere in London that implied that he had been dismissed. This seriously misleading piece of film could easily have damaged David's long-term career and certainly has made me more suspicious of documentaries on any topic. Happily David (a long-time friend of Marwell and one-time trustee) was headhunted for the directorship of the prestigious North Carolina Zoo where he has been very successful.

The dissent born of the financial crisis and the awakened interest of the Fellows of the Society was destined to be a factor in the rest of my involvement with the ZSL. Some Council meetings were fraught, as various members sought to advance their own views and positions. At the height of the crisis Council took the decision to close London Zoo. This was taken reluctantly, but rightly at the time because we were almost certainly very close to trading illegally by knowing that we were incurring liabilities that we might not be able to meet. Council members as trustees were legally responsible. All but one member voted for closure.

Those who had sought solutions when I first joined, such as Lord Peyton who had struggled so heroically to seek funding from government and other sources, departed when, in response to pressure, there was some likelihood of retraction of this resolution. In the event, a series of opportune gifts made closure of London Zoo unnecessary but it was a close call, and I look back to the traumatic meeting at which that decision was made with awe.

At Whipsnade we had to stop the financial loss and, as soon as possible, generate a surplus. This was not an easy task as there had been a long period of neglect of maintenance, and operating costs were totally disproportionate to the unacceptably low visitor numbers. This last problem was partly a lack of feeling that Whipsnade was part of the local community and not just the intellectual property of

171

a distant London body. This we sought to address both by changed marketing and by bringing local people on to the Board. Our task was not helped by the main restaurant being destroyed by fire early in Stuart's directorship. In time, but after many struggles with insurers, builders and planners, a magnificent suite of catering and function rooms was built, but for some time catering was limited with a predictable negative impact on income.

Initially, with the attention of the non-executive officers of the Society and most of the Fellows focused on London Zoo, we were left to our own devices, but as the Whipsnade board began to succeed and the threat of closure of London receded, there was (human beings being what they are) an inevitable push for a resumption of control from the centre and my strategy of effective independence won me disfavour in some areas, although not with the two Council members who were added to the Board, and who immediately saw at first hand what my strategy was achieving. I never sought independence from the Society for WWAP other than as a chance to establish its own marketing identity and with that a membership scheme that was directed to the community within its own visitor catchment area, together with the freedom to make crucial decisions, as needed, without fatal delay.

Most damaging to our recovery plan was the issue of contributions to central costs. Budgeting and financial control were well established within the zoo's resident staff, but had to be replicated at 'head office', as did personnel management. As we were really getting going, a Director General for the Society was appointed and I was told that he would have the ultimate authority and all the boards would be essentially advisory. At this point I resigned, having ensured that my successor would be Christopher Marler. I also had the opportunity to withdraw from Council as my three-year term coincided with that of one of London Zoo's stalwarts, J. Barrington Johnson. Each of us was prepared to defer to the other, but I chose to be the one to go, to the relief, I believe, of the president and some others who were already embarked on their own strategies. Barrie has since written an excellent *Story of London Zoo* to which I have had recourse in this account.

I am glad that I helped Whipsnade in its hour of need, but still feel that more could have been achieved had there been less desire for control from certain quarters. Sadly, during my time of close involvement with the ZSL it seemed incapable of harmonious progress. Academics always filled the positions of Secretary (the part-time and unpaid senior executive) and President (apart from Field Marshal John Chapple's short time in that post). The Society has often failed to keep the whole-hearted loyalty of staff and supporters that it needs for success. Since my active years, the Whipsnade Director with whom I worked has moved on and the ZSL has been led by three Director Generals.

As I write this some 12 years after my ZSL involvement, Chester Zoo is now in 2009 in many ways Britain's pre-eminent zoological institution. I now have no knowledge of how the ZSL is faring. As a Fellow of many years, I had no intention of not continuing membership when I ceased my commitments, and continued my banker's order although choosing not to visit either zoo. However, in August of 2003 I received a slightly wrongly addressed letter informing me that: 'Due to an error in our database we failed to write to you at the correct time to invite you to renew your Fellowship. This is regrettable and a mistake for which we apologise.' There was no need to 'invite' me to renew my membership which should have been renewed automatically and annually until I departed to that great zoo in the sky. To make matters worse the attached application form requested £98 from Fellows elected before 1996 (which of course I was) and £36 for those elected after 1996. I took no action!

Later I was happy to support a battle inaugurated by a director of finance at the ZSL and the Society's auditors, Ernst & Young. This was to fight for exemption from VAT on zoo admissions. My role was to agree to Marwell's contribution to a fighting fund and to encourage all the British charitably owned zoos to do likewise, as not all were hopeful of a satisfactory outcome. That outcome was very slow to come because HM Customs & Excise resisted our claims and, although they lost at every stage of a legal fight which went all the way to the European Court of Appeal, were even then slow to refund the substantial amounts due on VAT collected since 1990, plus interest. Furthermore they only remitted part of Marwell's entitlement because of the technicality already referred to that I had been both a Trustee and a paid Director. Although Marwell did not benefit from a refund to the extent that it should have done morally, all the charitably owned zoos had considerable windfalls and very great ongoing financial benefits from the ultimate victory. This was, of course, also very significant in ensuring the ongoing viability of both London and Whipsnade Zoos.

Chapter 14

One afternoon in Dublin in 1967, with a little time to kill between business meetings and my flight to London, I wandered down Grafton Street and into a shop that purported to research names and lineages for a modest amount of money. The result was a reasonably impressive (but probably as genuine as the proverbial $4 bill) coat of arms for my family name with the motto *Semper paratus* which I was informed means 'Always ready'. Genuine or otherwise, that motto does reflect the approach which I have always had to life. I have always been ready to take new ideas on board, listen to advice (although not always to take it) and to have a go.

Establishing a major zoo in Britain, with all the obstacles that I had to overcome, certainly called for being 'always ready'. Few days were predictable – life with animals is full of the unexpected. One day I could be in despair at the failure of a species in our care to breed, and almost immediately afterwards receive news of births. On another day I would be feeling pleased about a group, only to be told of some worrying health problem. I soon learnt that a zoo is like a human village in that, almost daily, there are births, deaths, accidents and sickness amongst the inhabitants.

There are also a large number of humans involved in the everyday life of a zoo. In addition to those involved in the care of animals there are at least an equal number with the diversity of skills needed to wrestle with endless paperwork, care for the infrastructure of buildings, fences and equipment, and oversee the marketing which aims to bring in that number of humans whose money makes the whole thing possible.

On a good visitor day in the summer we could have 4,000 visitors, and on a peak day such as a fine Easter Monday there could be nearly

10,000. Such numbers call for the skill of diplomacy from all staff members, beginning in the car park through to those at the entrance gate and then on to shop and catering staff. The keeping staff watch anxiously to see that our 'no feeding' rule is being obeyed and nothing is happening which might frighten their charges. In our later years we always had education staff members available to give talks and answer questions. Significantly, on peak days we benefited by an army of volunteers from the Marwell Zoological Society who helped in every non-animal department and also ran gentle fundraising activities to provide the zoo with ever-needed money for projects.

The great majority of our paying visitors were well behaved; only once was it necessary to call for police assistance, and even then the miscreants had left the zoo before the arrival of a squad car, encouraged no doubt by several of us following them in Park vehicles. This welcome absence of hooligan trouble was, I believe, due to the very obvious serious purpose of Marwell as well as admission prices which discouraged those elements of society who set out to cause mischief and damage. This is not to say that some of the public were not troublesome. Anyone who has not been involved with a visitor attraction would be amazed at the problems that have to be dealt with.

The greatest diplomats are the gatekeepers who patiently extract the right money from visitors whilst giving advice about the zoo itself and often about the local area as well. From its opening day Marwell has been remarkably well served by gate staff, many of whom were pensioners when they joined the team. Our first head gatekeeper stayed for many years and served Marwell brilliantly, but as he advanced into his eighties he became a trifle tetchy with awkward customers and I had to suggest that he should take honourable retirement. He took this rather badly, muttering that he had not realised that the post was temporary!

They all had stories of their encounters with visitors. One of the most frequent was when a family party would point to a child and say that he or she was less than three and therefore entitled to free admission, at which point the child would protest that it was at least five! Another of our veterans had language skills and responded in their own tongue to a party that he had overheard plotting to understate their children's ages.

Sometimes we were reminded of how little our urbanised visitors understood the natural world. I well remember a hot summer day when an irate lady found her way into my office and complained that she felt cheated of her money because the tigers were 'not doing anything'. My response was to offer her the loan of a stick and to escort her into the enclosure. She departed, raining such imprecations on my head that it is a wonder that I have survived.

Shortly after the birth of Marwell an anti-zoo organisation was formed in Britain calling itself Zoo Check which became a subsidiary of another registered charity called Born Free, named after the book and film about lions in Kenya. Both were and are dedicated to the closure of all zoos, and discussion with them, as I and other members of the zoo community soon discovered, is pointless – they are fanatically committed to the belief that all zoo animals suffer, to a greater or lesser degree, privation compared to their fortunate fellows roaming at will. At least that is the illusion that sustains their existence.

Anyone who has experienced the true (but shrinking) wild loves it, and wishes to preserve it and its inhabitants. We also know that a peaceful paradise it is not. There are accidents and illnesses and brutal territorial fights within species which in a good zoo are settled by skilful management and veterinary attention. Drought and famine do not threaten well-cared-for zoo animals. I have often said that if I was an animal within a group at Marwell being selected for a return to nature (and was able to be cognisant of what might be in store for me) I would seek a remote corner and hope to be overlooked.

In my experience, people who seek to work with zoo animals are lovers of animals as well as of nature. We would not choose to work with animals if financial reward was our goal! Zoo critics like to rubbish the role of saving species, saying that only a tiny percentage of Earth's threatened animals can be saved by zoos and so far only an even smaller number owe their survival to those institutions. Well, if only one were saved in my view that would be better than a little hand-wringing! In fact more have been saved, and not just the big and charismatic ones either. It is my fervent hope that my descendants will not have to live in a world without any creatures great or small that could have been preserved by *ex situ* breeding, even if my own species has made their *in situ* survival impossible.

Marwell in my time was remarkably well served by a loyal and dedicated staff. I was always ready to hear their views on whatever part of the zoo they worked in, and any other matter related to Marwell and wildlife. Today it seems necessary for even modestly sized operations to have one or more staff members responsible for what was once called 'Personnel' but now goes by the horrid title of 'Human Resources', which resonates to me of the slave trade! Apart from the few necessary meetings for operational planning I dealt with staff, preferably by meeting them at work during my tours of the zoo, at least a section of which I tried to do every day. Otherwise everyone knew that my door was always open for them unless I was away or locked into something from which I could not be disturbed. By modern management theory I was much too 'hands-on', but I can say with confidence that my way of doing things served me well during my times as a farmer and businessman and through to the building of a successful major zoo.

When in 1991 the Queen honoured me with an OBE for my 'contributions to conservation', I was conscious of the joke that says the letters stand for 'other b . . . . . . 's efforts' because I was blessed with wonderful support throughout most of my Marwell years by very supportive trustees and a staff which had only a very few dissenters. The latter were destined to have a ball when I finally left the Marwell scene!

After the nail-biting time seeking planning permission to have a zoo on the Marwell Hall estate and awaiting the outcome of the public enquiry, I enjoyed all of the years since receiving that blessed green light. This was despite the ever-present worry as I juggled money availability against needs. The thrill of a new species arriving and the never-ending joy of finding two animals where, before the magic of a birth, only one had been before, never left me. And notwithstanding the irritations sometimes caused by a certain type of visitor and their litter, it was a joy to know that our gentle mission to educate was appreciated and we were making converts to the cause of conservation.

The 1990s, however, were in many ways the best years. Economically, thanks to the sale of the hotel site, we were out of the clutches of our bankers and visitor numbers were increasing, thanks to word-of-mouth recommendation and the completion of the M3 motorway, prior to which people coming to us from the east and north-east of our visitor catchment area on summer weekends had to endure as long as two hours at the notorious Hockley traffic lights on the old Winchester bypass. This was not an experience that encouraged many repeat visits.

For most of the years of Marwell's life as a zoo open to visitors, Britain experienced a variety of economic crises which limited what the economists call the 'leisure spend', but these had at last diminished by 1993 when, in our 21st anniversary year, we welcomed over 340,000 visitors, which was the most to that date, and generated a surplus (also a record then) of nearly £348,000. A trickle of legacies was beginning to help finances as was the ever-growing fundraising of our support group, the Marwell Zoological Society. Legacies are a wonderful source of funds as they cause no pain to the departed beneficiary whilst leaving a lasting memorial to his or her interests and beliefs.

Lighter financial pressure enabled the Trust to move, as I have mentioned earlier, into conservation work overseas. Threats to British species were not ignored and off-exhibit breeding programmes were established with responsible local bodies for Sand lizards, Natterjack toads and Reddish buff moths, with progeny being released into suitable habitats.

My passion for Africa and its animals was not at the expense of those from other parts of our troubled planet. Indeed, my first loves, the Siberian tigers and the Przewalski's horses, are testament to a universal interest.

Gradually, as Marwell grew, animals from other continents were welcomed into our Ark. Early amongst these were engaging small primates from the diminishing rain forests of Brazil. These were marmosets, tamarins and Goeldi's monkeys. The distinction between the first two families relates to their different tooth structures, whilst the latter are regarded as 'true monkeys'. In 2005 we had eight species of these small animals housed either in large, well-branched cages or on islands. All had heated indoor accommodation and bred well in their family groups. Golden lion tamarins born at Marwell joined animals from a number of zoos for a training programme under the auspices of the Smithsonian Institution's National Zoo in Washington, prior to a successful release in Brazilian coastal rainforest. The Golden lion tamarins were close to extinction when Jersey Zoo's Jeremy Mallinson together with National Zoo staff initiated a co-operative captive breeding programme which included nearly all the animals then in zoos. They are now thriving both *in* and *ex situ*.

I first became aware of these small animals whilst leafing through a magazine in an American airport and seeing advertisements for 'living toys'. It is almost unbearable to imagine the tragedies that must have resulted from these sales. Perhaps it is because we humans are also primates that there has so often been a desire to add another species to our households. Such additions have almost always ended in tragedy for the animals, and sometimes for the owners.

I have never strayed east of Africa to the island of Madagascar, which is generally regarded as one of the worst areas of ecological destruction on earth. The island, which is believed to have been separated from most of the rest of Earth's land masses early in our planet's history, is home to a group of primates that are called prosimians. These are our modern-day lemurs, frozen in evolutionary time but now threatened by the expanding human population of a country with few natural resources. Marwell's World of Lemurs, built in the Hall's former kitchen gardens to which I have already made reference, became home to five lemur species and a little later to Madagascar's largest predator, the rather dog-like looking Fossa.

From Asia came the Siamang gibbons whose vocalisations carried as far as the village of Twyford several miles to the north and whose aerial gymnastics were constant crowd-pleasers. The Pacific island of Sulawesi has an indigenous monkey known as the Sulawesi crested macaque, which is critically endangered in its homeland but is prospering so well in zoos that breeding has to be limited. Marwell's present group is housed on the island which the train track encircles which, for their comfort, has a bridge arrangement that allows them to choose between a warm dry area or the bracing Hampshire air and the stares of the visitors. When first introduced to their new home there was a mass escape. Most were recaptured without too much difficulty but the boss male took the opportunity to inflict a severe bite on the leg of a keeper who had once squirted him with a water hose.

The addition of bats to Marwell with a walk-through house was the result of another 'off the top of my head' response to an architectural problem. I wanted to extend the stables for our Grevy's zebras in order to maintain what I felt we needed as a long-term viable number of breeding females. This was easy, as all that had to be done was to add some loose boxes to the existing range. However, from the rear this range looked distinctly stark so to break up the building line we built a bat house and added endangered Rodriguez fruit bats and Seba's short-tailed bats.

The opportunity to acquire a very large greenhouse from the liquidators of the Windsor Safari Park for a modest sum of money enabled us to build a tropical house on the site of part of the former stable block. Intended to house reptiles, amphibians and invertebrates amongst lush tropical vegetation, this brought a whole new dimension of animal viewing to a zoo which, with the exception of the giraffe and okapi houses, had previously been an open-air experience for our visitors. Opportunities to come out of the rain and cold on a high proportion of British days are an important part of providing visitor satisfaction. It was also a new dimension of animal keeping. Many of us have a natural empathy with warm-blooded creatures from which come natural responses to their needs. The brilliant Poison arrow frogs and the Red piranhas are less easy to warm to, but all responded to the care of head keeper Geoff Webb whose hobby was the care of small, cold-blooded animals. A colony of Leaf-cutter ants probably contained as many individuals within its clear plastic world as all the rest of the zoo. Certainly the colony's endless procession of worker ants carrying pieces of leaf in the manner of soldiers with banners is an intriguing sight. Most of the animals in the tropical house have complex life and reproductive systems which call for more explanatory graphics than for mammals, and these were supplied by our creative educators who also created a large entrance picture which very graphically depicted the effects of rain forest destruction.

From its very beginning Marwell had wildlife-related education as a major part of its mission. I always felt that the cause of conservation needed the support of that species which was the cause of its problems, namely human beings, and that support would only be forthcoming through knowledge. By information such as signs and quality guide books we reached very many visitors, but to get to the youngsters who would soon inherit the planet more formal classroom-type exposure was a duty of all zoos.

From the time that an Education Department was begun, thanks to the Manpower Services funding scheme, we had a succession of enthusiastic and talented education officers who did sterling work, attracting ever-increasing numbers of school children of most age groups, but operating in the quite unsuitable ground-floor rooms in Marwell Hall, a handicap made worse by them having to surrender these for the economically important, but very disruptive, annual Winter Wonderland. A purpose-built education centre was an ever-more urgent necessity which finally became a realistic hope by the mid-1990s when I and the trustees were confident that we could fund half the cost of such a building if only we could find a source for the other half. The National Lottery fund seemed to be a more than likely source. Our need was exactly what the Lottery was established for. Our architect met with the senior education staff and me, and as a result plans for a first-class facility were defined and a building designed which would meet all our needs and would be of such environmentally friendly construction that it could be a lesson in itself.

Informed that the Lottery Commission expected a very thorough submission, together with the already assembled internal team, we commissioned a division of KPMG to assist, and together, after a great deal of hard work, and a not insubstantial fee to KPMG, we produced a document which made an irrefutable case for Lottery money. Or at least that was what we thought! The dispensers of the nation's 'community benefit' money, garnered from those of our fellow citizens who hoped that their weekly purchases would prove to be a ticket to an easy life, thought otherwise. We learnt that there was no mechanism for appeal or dialogue.

There then began a chain of events which to this day I find amazing. Marwell Trustee Professor Norman Maclean arranged for me to meet with a consultant who advised Southampton University on possible funding sources from within the European Community. This courteous man listened sympathetically to my story and after a great deal of thought suggested what he described as an 'outside chance'. This was a fund called Konver (I cannot remember what this was an acronym for) which was established to generate employment in areas where jobs were being lost because of reductions of military activity. Fortuitously for us, although not for the military, this was happening with Navy establishments within our county of Hampshire.

Clutching at this straw of hope I persuaded the KPMG consultants to allow modest changes to be made to the Lottery document at no extra cost, and posted it off without great hope. One of the very few occasions in my life when I can truly say that I was bowled over by the contents of a letter was when I read that Konver was prepared to support our dream. I called Sally Millar, then our Head of Education, to my office and quietly handed her a piece of paper that said that her hope of many years was now about to become a reality.

Immediately an application for planning permission was made. Predictably, a few Owslebury residents made some difficulties which were overcome at a site meeting after I made one painful concession. An ideal site had been chosen which was close to the zoo's service gate and fitted snugly into a wooded area within the perimeter fence. I had wanted a small car park outside the service gate so that the 150 seating capacity theatre could be used for evening Zoological Society and other educational meetings without the difficulty of bringing people along the Park's internal roads, which was always a security risk. So many objections were made that an uninformed bystander might well have thought that I was proposing a casino . . . or worse! To avoid long delays I gave in, but I still feel annoyed that after so many years of good stewardship this was necessary, because of petty objectors.

Building work commenced in July 1998 shortly after my retirement from the Directorship in April of that year. By that time I was 68 years old and although I did not feel it, and every dawning day was as fresh and exciting as ever, I felt that I had a duty to what I had created to ensure that it would not be imperilled by anything that might happen to me. I moved from being the Director (I always preferred that traditional title for zoo bosses to the fancier ones now so often employed) to Honorary Director, retaining my role in conservation activities outside the Park.

My first successor, Dr Miranda Stevenson, resigned after some two years and has since become very successful as Director of the British & Irish Zoo Association of Zoos & Aquariums (BIAZA), formerly the Federation of Zoological Gardens of Great Britain & Ireland. It was then that I returned to the full-time post of Director until, after an extensive number of interviews, Mark Edgerley, until then Vice-Chairman of the Marwell Preservation Trust (MPT), assumed the Directorship. When he resigned, Lynne Stafford, whose career at Marwell had begun in July 1986 when she became my secretary, and who by her own talents and commitment to Marwell had risen to become Deputy Director, took the reins as Acting Director, a post which she managed extremely well until James Cretney was appointed as Chief Executive in July 2005.

Looking back to that time I can see that the then board of trustees was developing a feeling that the 'Knowles influence' was something to be reduced or eliminated. The new chief executive, who did not come from the world of zoos and conservation, had been appointed with the help of headhunters and, I suspect, was led to believe that Marwell needed major business surgery. Initially I was able to assist him by showing him exactly where the Marwell boundaries were and donating land, then still in my personal possession, to the Trust. I facilitated the merger of the Society and the Trust, which was a logical step forward by this time with Marwell's improving finances, and inaugurated an Ethics Committee which had then become a requirement for a licence to operate a zoo.

For many years I had enjoyed a happy and constructive relationship with the two chairmen who served throughout my directorship of the Trust, beginning with Tim Walker who took that office at the time of the Trust's formation and held it until his tragic and premature death in 1988, and then with Nick Jonas who stepped into that unexpected breach and filled it supremely well. Trustees served for three-year terms which were renewable at their expiry date, with the provision that they retired at the end of a term in which they became 70 years old. This meant that by 2006 Nick Jonas had retired, and although he was made President because of his great support, this was a non-voting post. Also gone by this time were all of the trustees who had supported me through good and bad years and blessed me with their faith.

Naively, I believed that the newer trustees, many of whom I did not know well, would still believe in my judgement and have some respect for my views. Sadly I was very wrong. At the last trustee meeting which I attended, James Cretney made it clear that Lynne Stafford was to be jettisoned and that he intended to surround himself with a new team in every non-animal department.

At that meeting I realised that, to put it plainly, I too was part of a history destined to be swept away by 'modernity'. This feeling was soon reinforced when the board chose to support the views of a man whom I had nurtured from studenthood into the position of Head of Conservation and Wildlife Management, but who for some time had sought to escape my authority and destroy initiatives which I had espoused. This happened at a meeting which I could not attend, but to which I submitted a paper requesting, with sound reasons, that Marwell should continue to support my Swaziland initiative by sending one more shipment of Roan antelope to that country. In my absence the board was told that by so doing Marwell would violate guidelines imposed by the Roan studbook keeper and the European and World Zoo Associations, and Marwell should not discredit itself by so doing. The opportunity to fulfil one of the often-stated reasons for zoos breeding endangered species was denied. The board sent me a very clear message by supporting a staff member rather than myself.

In November 2006 I wrote to the then Chairman, James Weatherall, resigning my own and Margaret's connections from that which was the result of our life endeavours.

As the matter of the Roan reintroduction was considered of great importance to the whole European zoo community, Rotterdam Zoo convened a meeting to which the Roan studbook keeper and his Director, both from Hanover Zoo, were invited along with the Director of the WAZA and the Chairman and a member of the European Zoo Association's Giraffe & Antelope Taxon Advisory Group. Hamish Currie and I represented Back to Africa, the charity which had facilitated the Swaziland project. After full discussion our project was vindicated and Marwell's reasons for declining continued involvement were proven unfounded. I communicated this to James Cretney and the (by then) new Chairman Simon Beloe, but received no acknowledgement, much less a retraction.

I am often asked by friends and former colleagues how I feel about my total severance from Marwell. My usual reply is that whilst I feel very disappointed by the lack of trust in my judgement shown by people who knew my record, I am also relieved that I took the decision to resign when I did, as I would not, had I still had a voice, have been able to remain quiescent whilst the 'new broom' swept away much that was my legacy. It is my fervent hope that the sweeping will be successful and that Marwell will go on to ever greater success. Anything else would be truly hard to accept.

After my retirement as Director I gave the Trust some of the land still in my ownership which was important for the fulfilment of my long-term plans for the zoo and its security. Most important of these gifts was what we had always called the Valley Field, a natural bowl-shaped area adjacent to the existing developed areas which was ideal for the development of an 'African bowl' containing a mix of grazing and browsing animals from that continent viewed from its perimeter by visitors either on foot or from a road train. To add to the drama I had plans for a large Lion enclosure to be so positioned that (as I had seen many years before in New York) it would appear that prey and predator were in the same area, although the animals would be well aware that this was not so. My plans were to blend this in to the existing zoo in which a new restaurant would be built so as to be readily accessible to visitors to both the new and established areas, and would be on a level site so important to the costs of building.

I believe that developments in that beautiful area are taking place, but in very different ways to those of the vision that I cherished for so long whilst awaiting only the necessary finance. Subsequent to the ending of my ties to Marwell I sold it some further land and buildings which the trustees felt that they needed. I left behind a ship in very good shape. Visitor numbers had increased to over half a million by 2005 which, together with the winning of the VAT battle, legacies and the (probably unintended) substantial benefit of Gift Aid on income from visitors, left the Trust with a surplus of in excess of £1.5 million. This is a long way from my struggles in the 1980s to achieve any surplus!

I look back on my achievements with pride. I appreciated being honoured by the Queen and was delighted to receive an Honorary Doctorate of Science from Southampton University in 2000 and another for Business Administration from Southampton Institute in 2001. I enjoyed the honour of having three visits from the Princess Royal, whose genuine interest in and wide knowledge of wildlife made all whom she met her committed admirers. Most of all I value approval by my peers, and look with pride at a certificate on my office wall recording an award by the Federation of Zoological Gardens of Great Britain & Ireland (the forerunner of the BIAZA) for 'outstanding achievement'.

I remain passionate about zoos and believe that the future will call on them to play an ever-greater role in ensuring the survival of species. Already, in 2008, zoos throughout the world are co-operating to raise money and provide staff and facilities to meet a crisis affecting many species of amphibians. Species survival is recognised to be equally important for small animals and not only the large and charismatic, as is sometimes suggested by misguided folk who have dedicated their lives to the extinction of zoos.

Way back in my poultry breeding days, I shared a concern with Bobby Cobb, the president of the American company, about the food and human population imbalance so obvious even then. Our concerns were not only commercial, as we looked into the potential benefits of improved husbandry for other animals. Bobby had humanitarian concerns and mine were for wildlife. He gave me a copy of a book by two brothers entitled *Famine 1975* which sought to destroy the then current beliefs that the famine which they predicted could be avoided. It was avoided, but hunger has persisted for many humans. Now the world has just emerged from a time when there were considered to be surpluses of food, and farmers were being paid to allow their land to lie fallow. There is once more recognition of an ever-growing demand from a still-growing population, and in Asia, increasingly people who are able to demand better levels of nutrition.

During the time of perceived food surpluses, many wild species were able to recolonise land not in use for crops or livestock. In Southern Africa commercially run parks were stocked with wild animals for tourists or hunters as a more profitable land use. They became, in fact, enormous zoos and have great value for ensuring the survival of many species. There is a risk that the present world economy crisis will reduce tourist travel, whilst increasing demand for food leads to a change of land use to the detriment of wildlife. The familiar competition for resources between humans and all organisms that are not of benefit to them has never ceased, but is likely to intensify.

I know that after the changes that took place since the beginning of the second half of the 20th century, our ongoing, modern zoos are well equipped philosophically, scientifically and collaboratively to play a major role in species survival. What is more, modern zoos are for people to enjoy leisure visits with no fear of exposure to the many undesirable aspects of modern life, whilst learning about the wonders of nature. Conditions have never been better for the animals in their care.

I am proud to have played a part in the evolution of zoos as well as the creation of one.

Index